UNDERSTANDING

THE
STALLION

YOUR **GUIDE** TO HORSE HEALTH
CARE AND MANAGEMENT

Also available from Eclipse Press

UNDERSTANDING

THE
STALLION

YOUR **GUIDE** TO HORSE HEALTH
CARE AND MANAGEMEN

E. L. Squires, PhD
Foreword by Norman W. Umphenour, DVM

ECLIPSE
PRESS

Essex, Connecticut

An imprint of Globe Pequot, the trade division of
The Rowman & Littlefield Publishing Group, Inc.
4501 Forbes Blvd., Ste. 200
Lanham, MD 20706
www.rowman.com

Distributed by NATIONAL BOOK NETWORK

Copyright © 1999, 2003 by Blood-Horse Publications
First Eclipse Press edition published 2023
Published by arrangement with the Thoroughbred Owners and
Breeders Association, Lexington, Kentucky

British Library Cataloguing in Publication Information available

Library of Congress Cataloging-in-Publication Data Available

ISBN 978-1-4930-7736-6 (paper : alk. paper)

Contents

Stallion management combines business and medicine in harmony with "Mother Nature." The evolution of the Thoroughbred industry has gone from racing, where winning a bet was the ultimate goal, to auctions, where the sale of million dollar yearlings is commonplace. Where once a gambler could win as much as the owner of the Kentucky Derby winner received from the purse, now races have purse money in the millions of dollars and the number of million-aire horses grows every year. This, in turn, drives up the value of stallions retiring to the stud.

Mare reproduction and management have always taken precedence over that of stallions, because many old horse-men considered that the mare contributed over 60% or more of the equation to produce the high-dollar offspring and champions. However, over the past 20 years as the price of stud fees has risen, the management and breeding of stallions has become a lucrative business. Because of this tremendous increase in earning potential there has been a great demand for the basic knowledge of stallion management! As with any business, good management is essential.

The management of stallions in such a way to obtain their maximum potential and efficiency has become critical. In order to compete for and afford the top stallions, farms have increased the number of mares in a stallion's book. Sending stallions to the Southern Hemisphere has also become a common practice. Outside the Thoroughbred industry, the transportation of frozen and cooled semen has become popular. Every one of these practices demands good and detailed management for the success of the endeavor. The cost both for the stallions themselves and for overall operating expenses must be cautiously monitored. However, without regard to the health and well-being of these animals, none of this could be possible. A horse must be healthy both physically and mentally in order to perform on a regular basis. Frequently, he must perform every day, several times a day, for the length of the breeding season. This is not unlike having to get to the racetrack everyday.

The chapters of *Understanding the Stallion* give both stallion managers and veterinarians the basic guidelines that they need to help cope with the day-to-day management of stallions. It is most important that we realize and strive to stay as close to "Mother Nature" as possible in understanding and dealing with the physiology, nutrition, exercise, and behavior of the breeding stallion. This book is an excellent reference for all who are involved in the management of stallions simply because it gives us a baseline from which to work. The knowledge that the author has gained, both professionally and personally in his career, gives readers of this book what the industry calls "a leg up."

Norman W. Umphenour, DVM
Ashford Stud
Versailles, Kentucky

INTRODUCTION

It has become obvious, after 23 years of teaching equine reproduction to breeders and veterinarians, that knowledge of proper stallion management lags behind that of mare management. This is partly due to a lack of information about the stallion that can be presented to the breeder and veterinarian. In addition, since there are more mare owners than stallion owners in each breed, most breeders and veterinarians have more experience with the mare than with the stallion. It seems as though many breeders do not set out to be stallion owners and stallion managers, but through numerous circumstances they end up owning a stallion.

The purpose of *Understanding the Stallion* is to provide an overview of reproduction in the stallion. This includes information on the anatomy and physiology of the stallion, as well as details on proper care and management. Factors affecting reproductive performance of the stallion also are included, since they are an important part of overall stallion management. My goal is to provide practical information not only to the reader considering purchasing his or her first stallion, but also to those that have been in the business of handling stallions for years.

Much of the information presented in this book was based on the Colorado State University bulletin "Management of the

Stallion for Maximum Reproductive Efficiency," written by me and B. W. Pickett, R. P. Amann, A. O. McKinnon, and J. L. Voss. Credit also goes to the experiences gained through working with Dr. B. W. Pickett over the past 23 years. The feedback from thousands of breeders and veterinarians who have attended our equine reproductive management short courses over the past 30 years have been the stimulus for much of the information presented on stallion management.

E. L. Squires
Professor, Department of Physiology
Equine Reproduction Laboratory
Colorado State University

CHAPTER 1

Reproductive Physiology of Stallions

In order to manage stallions properly, stud managers and veterinarians must have a basic understanding of the structure and function of the stallion's reproductive organs. In simple terms, the male reproductive system consists of a factory (testis), finishing school for spermatozoa (head and body of the epididymis), warehouse for the sperm (tail of the epididymis), and a delivery system (penis).

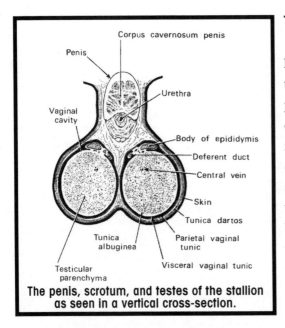

The penis, scrotum, and testes of the stallion as seen in a vertical cross-section.

TESTES

The testes of the stallion have two main functions: to produce sperm and to produce testosterone and other hormones. In normal stallions, the testes descend into the scrotum shortly before birth or within two weeks after birth. The scrotum provides protection to the testes and serves as a thermoregulatory mechanism. In order for spermatogenesis to proceed normally, the testicles must be exposed to a temperature several degrees below that of body temperature.

Underlying the skin of the scrotum is the tunica dartos, a layer of smooth muscle fibers, intermingled with connective tissue. This body of muscles has an important function in assisting in lowering and raising the testicle, depending upon environmental temperature. The external cremaster muscle also assists in regulating the position of the testicles.

The spermatic cord extends from the abdomen to its attachment on the testes. It suspends the testis in the scrotum and acts as a passageway for the deferent ducts, nerves, and blood vessels associated with the testes. The spermatic cord includes the highly coiled testicular artery. The veins draining the testes form a network of small veins around the highly coiled artery. This network of veins is called the pampiniform plexus and serves to cool the temperature of blood entering the testicle.

All of these thermoregulatory mechanisms are extremely important to maintain proper sperm production. Any elevation in temperature of the testes, due to either an elevation of body temperature or insulation of the scrotum due to swelling, will cause a disruption of normal sperm production. Thus, stallions should be monitored very closely for any sign of elevated body temperature or any swelling to the scrotum.

The testicular tissue minus the capsule, termed parenchyma, consists of two components: seminiferous tubules and interstitial tissue. The seminiferous tubules are lined by seminiferous epithelium that consists of different types of germ cells and the Sertoli cells. Leydig cells, which produce testos-

---

AT A GLANCE

• Sperm production occurs year-round and requires approximately 57 days.

• Elevated body and/or scrotum temperature can disrupt sperm production.

• It can take up to two months for normal sperm production to resume after trauma to the testis.

• Sperm production in a normal stallion decreases nearly 50% during the non-breeding season.

terone, are the major component of the interstitial tissue. The most immature form of germ cells (spermatogonia) line the basement membrane of the seminiferous tubules and Sertoli cells extend toward the lumen in a radial pattern. The Sertoli cells are termed "nurse" cells in that they are essential in providing nutrients to the developing germ cells. Convoluted seminiferous tubules lead to the straight portion of the seminiferous tubules. The straight tubules converge in the cranial

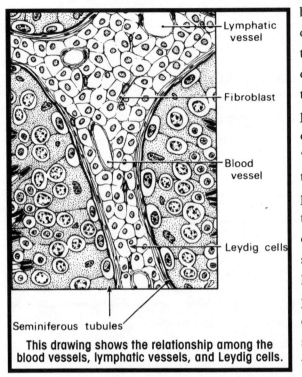

Lymphatic vessel

Fibroblast

Blood vessel

Leydig cells

Seminiferous tubules

This drawing shows the relationship among the blood vessels, lymphatic vessels, and Leydig cells.

two-thirds of the testis in an area termed the rete tubule. Each rete testis fuses with one of the 13 to 15 efferent ducts that lead to the epididymal duct. The epididymal duct then leads to the proximal part of the epididymis.

Leydig cells, within the interstitial tissue, produce a variety of steroid hormones, of which testosterone is a major hormone secreted by the stallion's testis. Other steroid hormones include androgens and estrogens. Concentration of testosterone at the level of the testicle is approximately 45 to 55 times higher than that in the jugular vein.

EPIDIDYMIS

The epididymis is divided into the head or caput, body or corpus, and tail or cauda. The head curves around the testis and the spermatic cord and continues as the body of the epididymis. The head is rather flat, whereas the body of the epi-

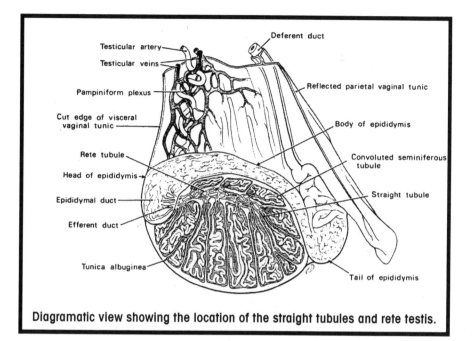

Testicular artery

Testicular veins

Pampiniform plexus

Cut edge of visceral vaginal tunic

Rete tubule

Head of epididymis

Epididymal duct

Efferent duct

Tunica albuginea

Deferent duct

Reflected parietal vaginal tunic

Body of epididymis

Convoluted seminiferous tubule

Straight tubule

Tail of epididymis

Diagramatic view showing the location of the straight tubules and rete testis.

didymis is cylindrical and the tail of the epididymis is a large, bulbous structure attached to the caudal pole of the testis. Efferent ducts plus the initial head of the epididymis are involved in resorption of fluid and possibly secretion of compounds. In the body of the epididymis, sperm maturation occurs and spermatozoa gain the ability to be fertile and motile. The tail of the epididymis stores approximately two-thirds of the spermatozoa. The tail contains sufficient number of spermatozoa for several ejaculates. Movement of spermatozoa through the epididymis is by peristaltic contraction. Time required to move spermatozoa through the head and body of the epididymis is not altered by ejaculation. In contrast, the number of sperm stored in the tail of the epididymis is altered by ejaculation. Stallions which are sexually rested for several days have more spermatozoa stored in the tail of the epididymis. One misconception is that frequent use of a stallion will result in ejaculation of immature spermatozoa. Spermatozoa are produced continuously, regardless of ejaculation frequency. Sperm that are not ejaculated are eliminated during urination.

Sperm travel from the tail of the epididymis through the deferent ducts and into the urethra. The deferent ducts widen in the pelvic area to form structures called the ampullae. The ampulla also is a storage area for spermatozoa. However, since the ampulla is contained within the body cavity, sperm that are stored in the ampulla are exposed to higher temperatures and usually are of lower motility with higher morphological abnormalities. Some stallions do not routinely void excess spermatozoa in the urine and thus accumulate large numbers of spermatozoa in the epididymis, deferent ducts, and ampullae. Generally, ejaculates from these stallions contain large numbers of spermatozoa that are morphologically abnormal. These stallions must be ejaculated several times in order to obtain good quality semen.

ACCESSORY SEX GLANDS

The accessory sex glands of the stallion include the vesicular glands (previously termed seminal vesicles), prostate gland, and bulbourethral gland. The vesicular glands are paired glands that contribute the gelatinous (gel) material contained in the ejaculate. The amount of gel produced varies with season of the year and the individual stallion. More gel is produced during April to July than other times of the year. In addition, the amount of gel in the ejaculate depends upon the sexual stimulation of the stallion. Those stallions used to tease several mares prior to ejaculation will produce large amounts of gelatinous material. Function of the gel in the ejaculate is not truly known.

For artificial insemination, generally the gel is separated from the gel-free fraction and is not used for insemination. The prostate gland is a single, firm, nodular gland surrounding the urethra. The secretion of the prostate gland is thin and watery and possibly serves to cleanse the urethra during ejaculation and contributes to seminal plasma. The two bulbourethral glands are positioned on each side of the pelvic urethra. These glands contribute to the seminal plasma.

Collectively, these glands contribute most of the fluid to the ejaculate.

PENIS

The urethra is a long, mucous-secreting tube that extends from the bladder to the free end of the penis. The pelvic portion of the urethra is covered by thick muscle that contracts vigorously during ejaculation. The urethra terminates in a free extension called the urethral process. The urethral process protrudes beyond the end of the glans penis and sometimes becomes irritated during collection or breeding. It is important when washing the stallion before breeding to examine the urethral process to make sure there is no indication of trauma or laceration.

The penis of the stallion is termed a muscular cavernosus type which becomes engorged with blood during erection. The major component of the penis is termed the corpus cavernosum and the minor component is a bulbospongiosus muscle. Both of these muscles become engorged with blood during the erection process. Ejaculation in a stallion involves movement and deposition of the spermatozoa from the deferent ducts and tail of the epididymis, as well as fluid from the accessory sex glands into the pelvic urethra. Ejaculation is the actual expulsion of semen through the urethra. In a stallion, ejaculation occurs in a series of strong, pulsatile contractions (three to six) which have been termed "jets" of semen. The majority of spermatozoa are contained in the first three to four jets.

SPERM PRODUCTION (SPERMATOGENESIS)

Stud managers and veterinarians must have a thorough knowledge of the events of spermatogenesis. Production of sperm is a continuous process throughout the year and requires approximately 57 days. Spermatogenesis is the sum of cell divisions and cellular changes that result in formation of spermatozoa from the most immature sperm cells, spermatogonia. The different types of germ cells are spermatogonia, primary spermatocytes, secondary spermatocytes and spermatids. If one looks at a cross-section of a normal seminiferous tubule, four or five generations of developing germ cells are arranged in a well-defined cellular association. Formation of a spermatozoon starts near the basement membrane where spermatogonia divide to form other spermatogonia and, ultimately, primary spermatocytes that are moved to a position from the basement membrane. A junctional complex between adjacent Sertoli cells forms a blood-testis barrier, which divides the seminiferous epithelium into two functional components: a basal (lower) compartment and an upper compartment. Primary spermatocytes are moved from the basal compartment through the junctional complexes into the upper compartment where they eventually divide to form secondary spermatocytes and spherical spermatids. The spermatids elongate and are eventually released into the lumen of the seminiferous tubules as spermatozoa. When released as spermatozoa, a major portion of the cytoplasm of each spermatid remains as a residual body, termed a cytoplasmic droplet. These droplets generally are extruded during passage through the head and body of the epididymis.

Knowledge of time required to produce a spermatozoon is essential for understanding the time course of events after drug injection or trauma to the testis. An interval of at least two months could be required for restoration of normal spermatogenesis after trauma to the testis. For example, if a stallion experiences an elevated temperature for several hours, quality of the spermatozoa in the ejaculate might be altered within a few days. This is attributed to damage of sperm within the epididymis. If the number and quality of spermatozoa in the ejaculate continues to be altered, this could reflect damage to the developing germ cells. If damage occurs at the level of the spermatogonia, then at least two months will be required before the quality and quantity of sperm in the ejaculate are improved.

Daily sperm production is the number of spermatozoa produced per day by a testis or the two testes of a stallion. Efficiency of sperm production is the number of sperm produced per gram of testicular tissue. During the breeding season, efficiency of sperm production is reasonably similar for normal stallions, although testicular size can differ greatly among stallions. Consequently, sperm production can be estimated with fair accuracy by measuring testis size. Because testis size increases as the stallion grows from two or three years of age to a sexually mature stallion, daily sperm output also increases.

Daily sperm production also is affected by season, with nearly a 50% decline during the non-breeding season in mature stallions. Efficiency of sperm production in a stallion decreases during the non-breeding season. This is especially true of 13- to 20-year-old stallions. In the non-breeding season, the number of spermatogonia decreases, as well as the number of Leydig cells and Sertoli cells. Daily sperm production in the breeding season is approximately 19 million sperm per day per gram of testicular tissue and only 15 million sperm per day per gram of testicular tissue in the non-breeding season.

HORMONAL CONTROL OF REPRODUCTIVE FUNCTION

Proper functioning of the testicles and maintenance of sex drive is governed by hormonal secretion from the hypothalamus, pituitary, and testes. See the appendix for the diagram showing the interrelationship of the hypothalamus, pituitary, and testes. Gonadotropin-releasing hormone (GnRH) from the hypothalamus (a portion of the brain) travels through the portal vessels that link the hypothalamus and anterior lobe of the pituitary and stimulates release of luteinizing hormone (LH) and follicle-stimulating hormone (FSH) from the anterior pituitary. Luteinizing hormone stimulates the Leydig cells of the testes to produce testosterone. The four major functions of testosterone are to provide a hormonal environment for germ cells; travel back to the pituitary and hypothalamus, and inhibit through a negative feedback any further LH secretion; to maintain the function of the accessory sex glands; and to induce normal sexual behavior. Some of the testosterone is also converted to estradiol, which also has some role in maintaining sexual behavior in the stallion. Furthermore, testosterone stimulates the formation of androgen-binding protein (ABP) which is involved in transporting testosterone to the germ cells.

Follicle-stimulating hormone, also coming from the anterior pituitary gland, stimulates function of the Sertoli cells to provide nutrients to germ cells, as well as stimulating the carrier protein, ABP. FSH action on the Sertoli cells also includes the stimulation of the hormone inhibin, which travels back to the pituitary gland and inhibits any further FSH secretion. A second hormone produced by the Sertoli cells, activin, is involved in regulating FSH secretion by stimulating the pituitary to produce and release FSH. As noted, this delicate balance in hormonal secretion between the hypothalamus, pituitary, and testes is dependent upon the balance of hormones in the stallion's blood. Therefore, any alteration in hormonal levels in the stallion's blood may, in fact, upset the delicate balance and inhibit sex drive or sperm production. It is important that a complete knowledge of a stallion's hormonal profile is determined prior to injecting any hormone into the stallion.

Even foals show sexual behavior.

GROWTH TO MATURITY

Generally, colts are maintained on their mothers until a typical weaning time of four to six months of age. Young colts then are maintained in a group until possibly two years of age unless they are sold as yearlings or enter into a training program for racing or showing. The nutritional requirements for young colts are no different from that of fillies and should follow the requirements of the National Research Council for growing animals. This usually includes a balanced diet of roughage, grain, mineral mix, and salt.

One of the biggest challenges of raising young horses is preventing injuries. Although it is best to provide pasture for the young, growing horses so they can

Most foals are weaned at four to six months.

get plenty of exercise, it is important that the fencing is well constructed and maintained in order to minimize the chance of injury.

Proper handling of the young colt as a weanling can help greatly in later training. The young colt should be taught to stand to be caught, haltered, and led. He also should be taught to have his feet trimmed and handled.

Puberty in the stallion has been defined as the ability to produce an ejaculate containing at least 50 million spermatozoa of which 10% are motile. This has been shown to occur at approximately 15 to 24 months, depending upon the season of the year when colts were born. Those colts born early in the year might, in fact, acquire puberty in the following spring or summer, whereas those born later in the season may be closer to two years of age at the time of puberty. Certainly colts and fillies should not be housed together after one year of age, since there is a chance of the young colts impregnating the young fillies.

Proper handling of weanling colts is important.

Training the young stallion to breed is extremely critical. Stallions should be allowed to show aggressiveness, but should not be allowed to endanger any of the personnel. Typically, the young stallion is quite naive as to the breeding process. Many of the young horses will mount without an erection and might even mount the front of the mare instead of the rear. This requires that an experienced mare holder assist in positioning the stallion properly on top of the mare.

Young horses should not be disciplined harshly for making mistakes during the breeding process. Generally, once a stallion has experienced ejaculation during collection or breeding, he will gain confidence and, after a few matings, will complete the ejaculatory process with few mistakes. Once a stallion has learned the proper way to mount, enter the mare, and ejaculate, then the stallion handler can begin to discipline the stallion if needed. Often, personnel who handle stallions are afraid of the stallions and overcompensate for their fear by excessive discipline. The

Stallion handlers should be experienced.

stallion is generally capable of identifying handlers who have fear and might become even more aggressive. Thus, it is best for only the experienced and confident stallion handlers to be involved in the training process of the young horse.

CHAPTER 2

Breeding Soundness Examination

Every stallion should undergo a breeding soundness exam. These examinations test the physical and mental ability of the stallion to breed mares. The tests include assessing the quality and quantity of semen, as well as the libido and mating of the stallion. Furthermore, this examination could uncover any possible congenital defects and infectious diseases and be used to estimate the number of mares which can be booked to the stallion. Breeding soundness exams should be done anytime the stallion is:

• being purchased or sold.

• the first time the stallion enters a breeding program.

• anytime a reproductive problem is detected.

• prior to each breeding season to establish an estimate of the number of covers or artificial inseminations that can be conducted.

• any time lowered fertility is suspected.

• anytime it is desirable to increase the number of mares to be bred.

• when the stallion is suspected of harboring a pathogenic bacteria.

• when abnormal sexual behavior is displayed and to determine if the stallion has changed in his potential from the previous year.

TYPES OF BREEDING SOUNDNESS EXAMS

There are typically two types of breeding soundness examinations. One includes two ejaculates collected one hour apart from sexually-rested stallions. The second ejaculate collected one hour after the first should have approximately 50% of the spermatozoa as the first ejaculate. If the second ejaculate does not contain half the spermatozoa of the first ejaculate, then one or more of the following should be suspected: a) one ejaculate was incomplete; b) the stallion has abnormally low sperm reserves; c) the stallion's sperm reserves had been depleted; d) the stallion was very young and immature or suffering from age-related testicular degeneration; or e) the stallion was abnormally accumulating large numbers of spermatozoa in the extragonadal sperm reserves.

A more complete evaluation includes daily collection for 10 to 14 days. The first several days' collections are used to stabilize the sperm reserves of the stallion and the last three ejaculates can be used to estimate average daily sperm output for that stallion. This latter evaluation is more appropriate for pre-purchase evaluations and for giving

> ## AT A GLANCE
>
> • Every stallion should undergo a breeding soundness exam.
>
> • A novice stallion should be handled carefully during the exam.
>
> • Sperm quality is assessed based on the percentage of spermatozoa that are progressively motile and morphologically normal.
>
> • In a normal stallion, sex drive usually determines the number of mares to which the stallion can be bred.

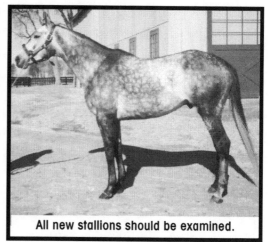

All new stallions should be examined.

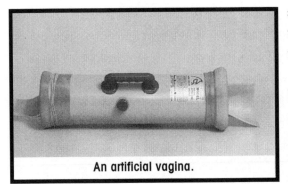

An artificial vagina.

an accurate estimate of the number of mares that the stallion can handle.

The requirements for a breeding soundness examination include an artificial vagina that elicits a favorable response and maintains the temperature of the semen, a tease mare which can be used to assess the sex drive of the stallion, and a phantom or live mare which is properly restrained for mounting by the stallion. In addition, the proper equipment for counting and evaluating the quality of the semen is essential.

BREEDING SOUNDNESS EXAM PROCEDURES

The stallion should be brought into the breeding shed and presented to a mare in estrus positioned behind a padded rail. Generally, the stallion should obtain an erection in a matter of a few minutes, although some novice stallions can take a lot longer and might, in fact, not obtain an erection on

A stallion presented to a tease mare.

the first session. These young stallions should be handled with extreme care and provided with whatever stimulus is necessary to obtain an erection. Once an erection is obtained, the stallion's penis is washed with warm water. At the time of washing, the penis is examined for any abnormalities. Teaching the horse to stand to be washed should be done with great patience and the washing procedure should be stimulatory to the stallion. If the stallion attempts to withdraw the penis, one should stop the washing procedure, tease the stallion again, and repeat the process. If care is taken when first training the stallion to be washed, then normal behavior can be established throughout the life of the stallion. One should examine the penis carefully during the washing process, particular-ly the glans and

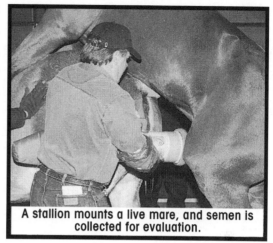
A stallion mounts a live mare, and semen is collected for evaluation.

urethral process for any signs of abrasions or sores. Once the stallion is washed, he is either presented to a live, hobbled mare or a phantom mare. Typically, the stallion should ejacu-late after only one or two mounts, depending upon the time of year in which the breeding soundness exam is performed.

There are three ways to discern whether or not ejaculation has occurred normally. Typically the stallion will flag his tail during the ejaculatory process and this can be used as an in-dication of ejaculation. However, it is also helpful to place the flat part of the hand on the base of the penis and feel the jets of semen being propelled through the urethra. Thirdly,

once the stallion comes off the mare, one can squeeze the end of the glans and, if a white, frothy secretion is present, this would indicate semen. A thin, watery secretion could indicate pre-sperm.

The stallion should be taught to come off of the mare and stand quietly so that cultures can be taken for possible isolation of bacteria. Cultures generally are taken from the prepuce, urethra,

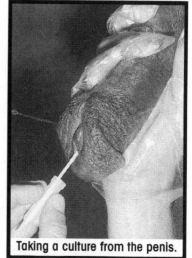
Taking a culture from the penis.

and semen of each ejaculate. The potential pathogenic bacteria generally associated with uterine infection include *Beta hemolytic streptococcus*, *Klebsiella pneumoniae*, *Pseudomonas aeruginosa*, and *E. coli*. The presence of non-pathogenic bacteria, such as bacillus and staph, are quite typical in a stallion's ejaculate. These generally are normal bacterial flora that are part of the reproductive tract. Isolation of one of the pathogens in several of the cultures certainly would be of concern, since these bacteria are capable of inducing uterine infection in mares after breeding or insemination. Fortunately, very few stallions are ever actively infected with bacteria, but are merely carriers of the bacteria. Thus, in an artificial insemination program, the easiest way of eliminating the bacteria is to treat the semen with extender containing antibiotics. Unfortunately, with natural mating, elimination of bacteria from the stallion is quite difficult and generally requires antibiotic treatment of the stallion.

Once the semen is collected, it should be taken into a clean laboratory and evaluated. The parameters measured include:

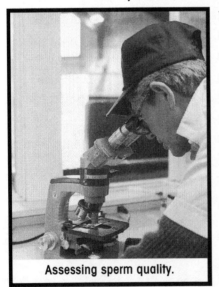

Assessing sperm quality.

volume of gel; gel-free and total seminal volume; concentration of spermatozoa per milliliter; total sperm in the ejaculate; percentage of progressively motile spermatozoa; percentage of morphologically normal spermatozoa; and testis size. The artificial vagina should contain an in-line filter which allows separation of the gel from the gel-free fraction. The filter can be removed from the collection bottle and the gel portion poured into a cylinder and measured. The gel-free fraction can be poured into a specimen cup or graduate cylinder and its volume determined. The volume of gel is not terribly important and varies tremendously from stallion to stallion and with season. Stallions that are teased heavily prior to collection will produce more gel and gel volume also is greatest during the middle of the breeding season.

The number of spermatozoa per milliliter of gel-free semen can be determined by several instruments. These include Spectronic 20 sperm counter (Bausch & Lomb), Densimeter (Animal Reproduction Systems), Spermicue (MiniTube Corp.), and HRI (Hamilton Thorne). An alternative to the automated system of counting sperm is the use of a hemacytometer in which the number of spermatozoa are counted on a slide. Regardless of the method used, the number of spermatozoa/ml must be obtained and multiplied by the volume of gel-free semen to determine the total sperm in the ejaculate.

Quality of the spermatozoa is assessed by evaluating the percentage of spermatozoa that are progressively motile and the percentage of spermatozoa that are morphologically

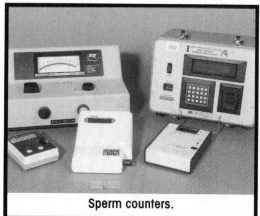

Sperm counters.

normal. Sperm should be diluted to approximately 20 to 25 million spermatozoa/ml in a skim milk extender for proper assessment of spermatozoal motility. Proper visualization of the sperm requires a phase-contrast microscope with a heated stage set at 37° C. The percentage of spermatozoa moving in a straight line is estimated. Notice also should be given to the total number of spermatozoa that are moving and the velocity of the sperm. A sample of raw semen should be used to compare with that of the extended semen. Typically, in undiluted semen samples, one observes head-to-head agglutination(or clumping) of spermatozoa which results in a swirling motion of a clump of spermatozoa. Thus, it is difficult to estimate percentage of progressively motile spermatozoa in undiluted samples. One also should examine the ejaculate of semen for the presence of any abnormal cells such as immature germ cells, white blood cells, or red blood cells. Certainly the presence of any of these abnormal cells is an indication of a problem. The two most important seminal characteristics of an ejaculate appear to be total sperm number in the ejaculate and percentage of spermatozoa that are progressively motile.

Another parameter of great importance is the percentage of spermatozoa that are morphologically normal. This is generally assessed by mixing the semen with a stain on a clean microscope slide and examining the spermatozoa under 1,000-times magnification. The percentage of morphologically normal spermatozoa should be at least 50% of the ejaculate and the

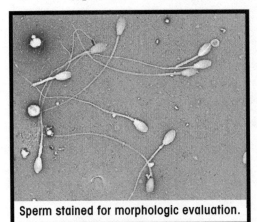

Sperm stained for morphologic evaluation.

percentage of progressively motile spermatozoa in a normal ejaculate should be in the range of 50% to 80%.

Pickett et all (1988) reported on breeding soundness examinations of 1,044 stallions between 1968 and 1987. These data were used to compare seminal characteristics and total scrotal width of stallions which "passed" a seminal evaluation to those which "failed." Additional data were obtained on seminal characteristics of stallions by breed, age, and month of the year. Overall, for stallions which passed, the average gel-free volume in an ejaculate was 45 ml, concentration 305 million/ml, total sperm/ejaculate 11 billion, and the percentage of progressively motile and morphologically normal spermatozoa was 53% and 51%, respectively.

The study indicated that daily sperm output appeared to increase sharply to five years of age, then remained essentially constant to 12 years of age. A total of 73 of the 1,044 stallions failed their seminal evaluation exclusively because a majority of culture sites were positive for either *Klebsiella*, *Pseudomonas*, or *Beta hemolytic streptococcus*. Of the 530 stallions which passed the biological portion of the breeding soundness examination, 154 (29%) had at least one culture positive for a potential pathogenic organism. However, the frequency of isolation or the level of growth was insufficient to warrant failing these stallions. *Klebsiella pneumoniae* was the most commonly isolated organism (68 stallions or 12.8% of the stallions).

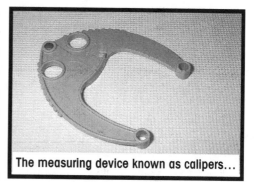

The presence of potential pathogens in the semen did not adversely affect any of the seminal characteristics or total scrotal width.

The measuring device known as calipers...

One of the most important parts of the breeding soundness examination is palpation and measurement of the stallion's testes. Each individual testis should be

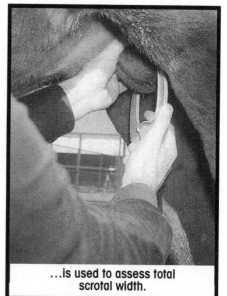

evaluated separately by placing the thumb on the lateral part of the testicle and the fingers on the medial portion. The testicle then should be slid between the hands and felt for any evidence of roughness, lobulation, or change in consistency such as extreme softness or firmness. The tail of the epididymis also can be felt at the caudal portion of the testicle; its size is

...is used to assess total scrotal width.

related somewhat to the sperm reserves of the stallion. If the tail of the epididymis is not located at the caudal portion of the testicle, then the testicle is probably rotated within the scrotum. Total scrotal width, as assessed by using calipers, is the best measurement for predicting sperm output of the stallion. The testicle also can be measured by using ultrasonography. A cross-sectional area through the widest portion of the testis can be determined, as well as the length. By using the formula, $4/3 \ \pi AC$, where A is the cross-sectional area and C is the length divided by 2 , testicular volume can be obtained. Once testicular volume is obtained, this can be placed into a formula to calculate the expected daily sperm output.

DETERMINING THE OPTIMUM NUMBER

Numerous factors must be taken into account when devising strategies to determine the maximum number of mares to which a stallion can be bred in a given year. There is no simple equation to calculate this number accurately. The components include the reproductive history of the stallion, age, testis size, semen quality, sex drive, and the method of breeding. Certainly, more mares can be bred with artificial insemination than natural mating. Furthermore, a knowledge of the previous reproductive performance of the stallion helps to predict further capabilities. Generally, if a stallion has normal-sized testes, the single limiting factor is sex drive. The type of mares presented to the stallion also can be quite important. For example, if a large number of

Age, sex drive, and other factors determine how many mares a stallion can cover.

barren mares are presented to the stallion, then perhaps more frequent breedings are needed to obtain pregnancies. Furthermore, if a large number of foaling mares are booked to the stallion, then these mares generally foal later in the season and might impose an additional stress on the stallion by having a large number of mares to be bred late in the season. The most advantageous situation is to have an

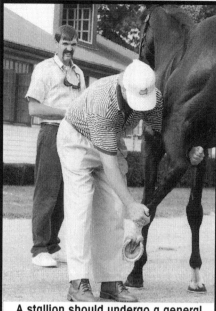

A stallion should undergo a general physical exam.

equal distribution of maiden, barren, and lactating mares.

It is important to obtain previous breeding performance of the stallion and any history of illness, injury, or medication. A general physical exam should be conducted to determine the overall condition of the horse and particularly to determine if there is any indication of lameness in the hind legs or back problems. The unwillingness to mount or the inability to complete the breeding process is sometimes associated with pain in the hocks or stifle or possibly the back.

REFERENCES

Pickett, BW, Voss, JL, Bowen, RA, Squires, EL, and McKinnon, AO. 1988. Seminal characteristics and total scrotal width (TSW) of normal and abnormal stallions. Proc. 33rd Ann. Conv. AAEP. pp 487-519.

Love, CC, Garcia, MC, Riera, FR, and Kenney, RM. 1991. Evaluation of measures taken by ultrasonography and calipers to estimate testicular volume and predict daily sperm output in the stallion. *J. Reprod. Fertility*, Suppl. 44: 99-105.

CHAPTER 3

Training the Stallion to Breed

Safety to the stallion and to the personnel is the most critical feature, whether the stallion breeds naturally or has semen collected for artificial insemination. Being kicked during the process of breeding is one of the major causes of low libido and abnormal sexual behavior. If the stallion is to mount a live mare, the mare should be properly restrained. In the Thoroughbred industry, where natural mating is most common, the type of restraint includes a chain shank, a nose twitch, and boots on the hind feet of the mare. In addition, it is quite common for the front leg of the mare to be elevated during the mounting process. Once the stallion is on the mare and she is standing quietly, then the front leg is lowered. Maiden mares experiencing their first breeding are often mounted by a tease stallion in order to discern the degree of receptivi-

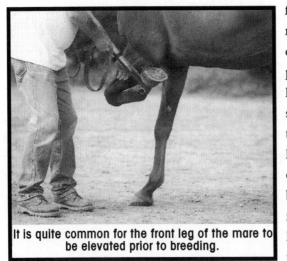

It is quite common for the front leg of the mare to be elevated prior to breeding.

ty. Once a mare is shown to be in good standing estrus, then the breeding stallion is allowed to mount.

Other types of restraint for the mare include a scotch hobble, in which a soft cotton rope is placed around the neck of the mare and the left leg is pulled forward such that the mare cannot kick during breeding. For semen collection and artificial insemination, generally the stallion is mounted on a docile "jump" mare. This mare has generally been selected for her willingness to be mounted during estrus. Hock hobbles are the preferred restraint used on the jump mare. A rope pulley that extends from the front legs to each of the hind legs allows the mare to move but prevents the mare from kicking the stallion during mounting. The ability to lead the mare while she is wearing hobbles is an advantage for stallions which have low sex drive. The additional stimulation of following a mare stimulates an erection and a produces a desire by the stallion to mount.

Having properly trained personnel in the breeding shed is ex-

AT A GLANCE

• A stallion kicked during breeding can develop low libido or abnormal sexual behavior.

• In the Thoroughbred industry, mares usually are restrained in some manner during breeding.

• Proper positioning of the stallion and mare is extremely important.

• Some stallions require extra stimuli before they will breed.

• A mare should be washed and her tail wrapped before breeding to prevent contamination to the stallion.

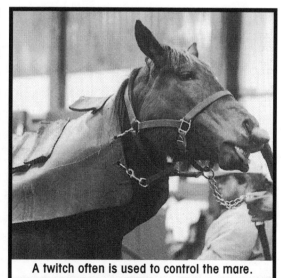

A twitch often is used to control the mare.

Maiden mares often are mounted by a tease stallion.

tremely important for safety and to accomplish the breeding process. Typically in a natural-mating program, there are one or two personnel who handle the mare, a stallion handler, and an additional person who assists the stallion in entering the mare. With artificial insemination, a mare handler, stallion handler, and collector are needed. Obviously if the stallion is mounted on a phantom mare, then this eliminates the need for a mare handler and the collection process can be accomplished with only two people.

PROPER POSITIONING

The proper positioning of the mare and stallion is extremely important. In pasture breeding of horses, it is quite common for the stallion to approach the mare's side and head to test the mare thoroughly before he moves to the

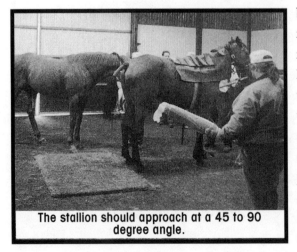

The stallion should approach at a 45 to 90 degree angle.

back of the mare and mounts. With hand mating, the stallion handler should allow the stallion to approach the mare from the side at about a 45- to 90-degree angle, or approach the mare directly from the rear. It is often dangerous if the stallion handler allows the stallion to go directly to the mare's head. One common mistake is for the stallion handler to have the stallion parallel with the mare, then pull the stallion toward him in order to separate the mare and

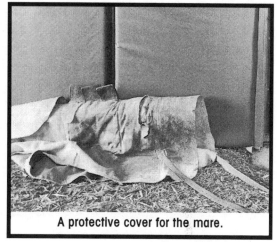

A protective cover for the mare.

stallion. This generally results in the stallion kicking at the mare, which could injure the mare and/or mare handler. The stallion should always be backed away from the mare, then presented to the rear of the mare and allowed to mount.

In semen collection for artificial insemination, the semen collector should orchestrate the collection process. If a jump mare is being used, the stallion handler should approach the mare from the rear and, upon being told by the collector that the stallion has an erection, the stallion should be allowed to mount. The collector then deflects the stallion's penis into the artificial vagina and collects semen.

For those stallions with low libido, allowing the stallion to approach the mare's side or front is sometimes stimulating. Other types of stimulation can include leading the mare slowly or placing another mare alongside the jump mare. If the stallion re-

An artificial vagina used to collect semen.

quires more than two mounts before ejaculation, then changes need to be made. This might include changes in the temperature and pressure of the artificial vagina or providing the stallion with another mare in estrus. Those stallions which readily obtain an erection and mount the phantom mare are certainly most desirable.

HANDLING THE STALLION

From my experience, the majority of stallions on large commercial breeding farms are handled with great care and skill. In contrast, stallions on smaller farms handled by personnel who are not used to dealing with stallions often are mishan-

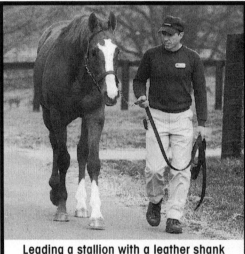

Leading a stallion with a leather shank and metal chain.

dled. Some typical mistakes include allowing someone to handle a stallion who shows obvious fear of the stallion. This either results in the stallion endangering the handler and personnel or, in some cases, over-correction and rough treatment of the stallion. The stallion should be handled with a 20-foot leather lead-shank that has a short portion of chain. The chain portion should be long enough to thread down one side of the halter and be connected to the ring on the opposite side of the halter. Place the chain in the stallion's mouth over the tongue. A slight tug on the stallion's shank will cause the stallion to pay immediate attention and respect the stallion handler. Certainly, one should not be overly aggressive with this method of restraint since it is possible to damage the mouth or tongue. Other handlers prefer to place the chain underneath the stallion's chin. This has the unfortunate disadvantage of causing the stallion to jerk and raise his head. The third option is to place the chain over the stallion's nose, which seems to be preferred by many breeders. However, if the stallion needs to be reprimanded severely during the breeding process, this could cause some damage to the bridge of the stallion's nose.

The stallion handler should allow the stallion to be aggressive and not discourage the stallion from bellowing or obtaining an erection. However, in no case should the stallion be allowed to endanger the handler or personnel. Correct positioning of the stallion handler is beside the stallion with contact between the handler's right elbow and the stallion's shoulder. The handler should not be in front of the stallion since this puts the handler in the position of being jumped on if the stallion bolts. If the stallion rears, then the use of a long stud shank will prevent the stallion from breaking away. Once the stallion lands, then the handler can gather the stallion and regroup. One common mistake is for the handler to pull on the stallion when he is in the air, which in most cases causes the stallion to rear higher and might in fact cause the stallion to fall over.

The best approach is to allow the stallion to obtain an erection prior to being presented to the mare. If, however, the stallion requires more sexual stimulus than just being in close proximity to the mare, then the stallion should be presented to the mare's buttock or flank area. If the stallion comes alongside the mare, the handler should be sure to back the stallion away from the mare prior to allowing the stallion to mount. Another common mistake is for the handler to pull the stallion away from the mare in a way that places the stallion's hind end against the mare. In most cases, the stallion will kick at the mare if he is in such a position. This certainly is dangerous and could cause harm to the mare or to the mare handler.

Stallions which have developed the bad habit of biting should be muzzled during the breeding process. The preferred type of muzzle is a leather muzzle that snaps onto the halter. This is much more preferable than continual jerking of the stallion's head to prevent him from biting at the mare. With the use of a muzzle, the stallion is still able to sniff and touch the mare, but not bite the mare or the stallion handler.

A muzzle to prevent biting.

In some extreme cases, it is necessary to decrease the stallion's visibility to the stallion handler. This is particularly true of stallions with abnormal sexual behavior or perhaps very young stallions which are disturbed easily by the movement of the stallion handler or collector. This is best accomplished by placing a set of blinkers on the stallion's head that focus the stallion's vision directly in front toward the mare and not toward the handler or collector.

Patience in proper training of the stallion will result in normal sexual behavior throughout the life of the stallion.

TRAINING TO A PHANTOM

Proper training of a stallion to mount a phantom mare is quite important. The ideal situation is for the stallion to be presented to a tease mare, obtain an erection, maintain the erection during the washing process, then immediately mount the phantom upon presentation. If stallions are taught the process of mounting a phantom mare and have been properly handled, these stallion will continue to mount a phantom mare and have semen collected throughout their reproductive life. Studies were conducted at Colorado State University to determine what percentage of stallions would mount the phantom. These stallions were mature stallions which had previously experienced collection of semen with an artificial vagina. The three treatment groups were: 1) presented to the phantom without any stimulus from a mare; 2) presented to a tease mare and, once an erection was obtained, presented to the phantom; and 3) presented to the tease mare and, upon obtaining an erection, the tease mare was placed parallel to the phantom mare. Five of 10 stallions in group 1, four of 10 stallions in group 2 and eight of 10 stallions in group 3 mounted the phantom and ejaculated the first time.

Training to the phantom should be done during the time that the stallion has the highest sex drive, which is generally in the middle of the breeding season.

Breeding to a phantom with a live mare nearby.

Although many breeders would like to train their stallions to the phantom prior to the breeding season, this is the time of year when sexual behavior is lowest. We would suggest that a stallion be presented to a tease mare and, upon obtaining an erection, be presented to the phantom. If, after several sessions, the stallion has failed to mount the phantom, then the tease mare should be positioned parallel to the phantom as an added stimulus. It is important that the stallion be positioned at an approximately 45-degree angle to the phantom and allowed to reach over the phantom and tease the mare. This generally results in the stallion becoming quite aggressive and, eventually, mounting the phantom. Generally the stallion rears up and must be directed on the phantom. If the stallion is positioned too far to the rear of the phantom, he will more than likely mount the tease mare and not the phantom. In many cases, once the stallion learns to mount the phantom and ejaculate on a regular basis, the tease mare positioned beside the phantom can be eliminated. However, if stallions are experiencing difficulty in mounting the phantom or difficulty in ejaculating, once mounted on a phantom, then occasionally positioning the tease mare beside the phantom can help.

It is commonly asked — What should one put on the phantom to make the stallion mount? The answer is nothing. Placing estrus mare urine on the phantom increases sniffing and flehmen, but does not encourage mounting.

PREPARATION OF THE MARE

Preparation of the mare for natural breeding or semen collection is important to prevent contamination of the stallion.

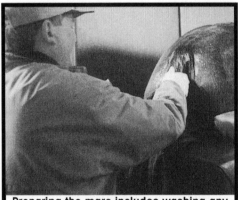

Preparing the mare includes washing any part the stallion might touch...

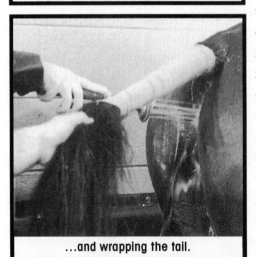

...and wrapping the tail.

For either natural mating or semen collection, the tail of the mare should be wrapped so that no tail hairs are visible. This can be accomplished using either gauze, leg wraps, velcro wraps, or tube socks. Generally, the material should be taped so that the wrap will not come off during breeding. The vulva and buttock area then should be washed with clean water or water containing a disinfectant such as an iodine solution. This can be accomplished using either cotton or paper towels. Any area where the stallion might touch the mare should be cleaned thoroughly. It is important to work from the lips of the vulva toward the outside of the buttocks. It is helpful if a string is tied to the mare's tail so that, once the stallion is mounted, the tail can be pulled away from the vulva area, thus assisting the stallion in entering the vulva or artificial vagina.

PREPARATION OF THE STALLION

For natural mating, the stallion is generally washed both before and after breeding. Excessive use of antiseptics or antibacterials should be avoided since overuse of these compounds results in destruction of the natural bacterial flora of the stallion's penis. Once this occurs, then opportunistic bacteria invade the stallion's penis. Generally, warm water is sufficient for washing the stallion prior to and after breeding. In an artificial insemination program, the stallion is only washed before the collection process.

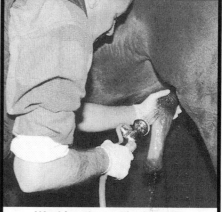

Washing the stallion's penis.

CHAPTER 4

Stallion Management

G eneral considerations for good stallion management are maintenance of the stallion in excellent health and a stress-free environment that will maintain normal sexual behavior and sperm production. Housing for the stallion is generally a matter of personal preference as to the size and type of construction. However, stallions should not be maintained in complete isolation, but should be able to see other mares and stallions. The type of housing used for stallions in Central Kentucky would appear to be ideal. The majority of these stallions are maintained in a stallion barn containing several stallions, but each stallion has its own paddock separated by double fencing from adjacent paddocks. This allows a stallion to have considerable exercise and interaction with other stallions.

Exercise requirements differ for individual stallions.

EXERCISE

The requirements for exercise vary considerably with each individual stallion. There are some stallions which, given the opportunity, will exercise freely to the point of weight loss. Other stallions which are more complacent and lazy might have to be force-exercised by lunging or a hot walker. Exercise is needed to maintain a stallion in good body condition so that he does not become too fat. Excess fat on a stallion will insulate the testicles and could affect semen quality. However, the major reason for exercise is to prevent boredom and maintain a good mental attitude and sex drive. Signs of boredom can include stall weaving, cribbing, and aggressive behavior. Some less-aggressive stallions can be maintained in a barn

> ## AT A GLANCE
>
> • A stallion should not be kept in isolation.
>
> • Exercise and dietary requirements depend on the individual stallion.
>
> • Stallions should have a breeding soundness exam every year, especially as they get older.
>
> • Management of older stallions might include reducing the frequency of breeding and the size of the book.

that also houses mares. At Colorado State University, stallions are housed in 12 x 12 stalls and alternate being turned out into 12 x 36 runs. Many farms invest significant money to ensure the safety and comfort of the stal-

A Central Kentucky stallion barn.

lion, as well as to provide attractive surroundings for promotion of their stallion.

NUTRITION

The nutritional requirements of the stallion vary depending upon the stallion's size, condition, work load, and tem-

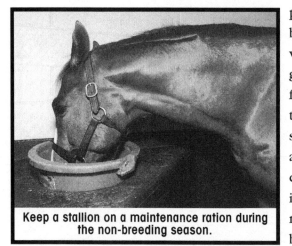

Keep a stallion on a maintenance ration during the non-breeding season.

perament. During the breeding season, the work load for a stallion is greater than that of a performance horse and therefore the stallion should be fed as an animal under heavy work conditions. This would include a good quality roughage at 2% to 3% of body weight, as well as 0.5% to 1% of a grain ration. An alternative would include adequate pasture supplemented by a good quality hay, grain, and salt and mineral mix. During the non-breeding season, the stallion generally can be maintained on a maintenance ration. Typically, breeding stallions are overfed instead of underfed, which could affect their sex drive and seminal quality. The need for vitamin supplementation has not been documented for the stallion. In fact, supplementation of vitamins A and E had no effect on sperm production. Stallions also should be placed on a routine vaccination and deworming schedule. It is important that the stallion be given proper hoof and dental care as well.

THE OLDER STALLION

It is difficult to define exactly when a stallion should be placed in the category of "older" since behavioral and testicular changes occur at various times in individual stallions. Some stallions are showing significant changes by 12 years of age whereas other stallions remain unchanged even at 20 years of age. It is critical that a thorough breeding soundness examination is performed on stallions each year, particularly as they get older, to determine if any significant changes occurred from the previous year. This information will allow one to manage a stallion properly during his mature years.

This might include a change in breeding frequency or number of mares that are booked to the stallion. The goal is to maximize the performance of the stallion each year.

One common problem in the older stallion is the inability to maintain good body condition. This might require the assistance of an equine nutritionist who could evaluate and perhaps fortify the stallion's diet so the stallion is more likely to maintain weight. It also might result in a change of housing so that the stallion does not exercise as vigorously. Another problem detected in mature stallions is sore-

Older stallions have special considerations.

ness in the legs and back that might impact their ability to breed mares. If a stallion is used in an artificial insemination program, this can be corrected by adjusting the height of the phantom mare so that the stallion is comfortable when mounted on the phantom. Horses with severe laminitis or hock problems might require a phantom lowered to a point where only the stallion's front legs are off the ground a few inches. Another possibility is giving the stallion a pain killer prior to the time of breeding.

Loss of libido in older stallions is not uncommon. This is typically true of stallions which have become sexually satiated toward the latter part of the breeding season. This could require a decrease in the stallion's book or a shortened breeding season. A stallion also might require more stimulus, such as several mares in estrus of various sizes and colors. There is always a great desire to enhance a stallion's sexual behavior with hormone therapy. As discussed previously, it is extremely important to analyze the stallion's hormonal profile prior to injection of additional hormones. Furthermore, consultation with a veterinarian is extremely important. With proper management, it is possible to extend the reproductive life of the mature stallion and allow him to perform to his maximum.

WHEN TO CASTRATE

Obviously, making the decision to castrate a stallion is an extremely important one. Generally, only a very small percentage of male horses should remain stallions if breeders

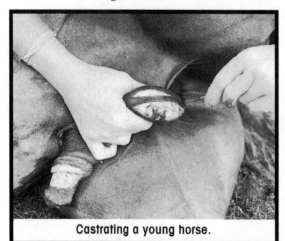

Castrating a young horse.

want to improve the genetics of the breed. Thus, very careful selection should take place in deciding which of the young colts to maintain as stallions.

Other considerations are the economics of maintaining a stallion. Once stallions experience puberty, they generally become quite aggressive and might need to be maintained in separate facilities. Certainly, they will need to be separated from mares. Some breeders who are not interested in showing or racing may decide to maintain their colts as a group in a pasture or paddock until they are several years old. The breeder always takes a chance that one of these young colts will become injured when they spar with their mates.

Once the breeder has decided that the young stallion is not of sufficient quality to be used as a breeding sire, then castration should be done immediately. Some breeders prefer to castrate their colts as weanlings, whereas others are more apt to castrate their colts as yearlings. The advantage of allowing the colt to reach 12 to 18 months is to allow further time for evaluation of the young stallion to determine whether he is truly a stallion prospect. In addition, it is sometimes easier to castrate a stallion as a yearling since his testicles are bigger and both are descended into the scrotum. Stallions used for showing or racing that display extreme aggressiveness during competition also could warrant castration. In addition, some racehorses that have large testicles experience pain during training and racing, possibly affecting performance.

The recuperation period after castration depends somewhat upon the age of the horse. Obviously, the younger the colt is castrated, the less traumatic the process and the quicker the recovery. However, generally it requires seven to 10 days for recovery from castration. It is important to provide the horse with exercise during this recovery period to minimize swelling to the scrotum. In addition, it is important to monitor the health and attitude of the castrated horse during this recuperation period.

One commonly asked question is, "Why do some geldings retain stallion-like behavior after castration?" This is often blamed on the veterinarian leaving a portion of the testicle within the scrotum. The term "proud cut" refers to a gelding in which part of the tail of the epididymis, or any portion of the epididymis, is left in the horse after the testicles have been removed. Contrary to some claims, the tail of the epididymis does not produce testosterone nor cause stallion-like behavior after castration. If the gelding continues to have stallion-like characteristics after castration, this is probably because of learned behavior that is not hormonally controlled. Generally, the older the stallion at castration, the more likely it is that the horse will retain some stallion-like characteristics after castration. These stallion-like characteristics will more than likely subside a few months after castration. However, it is possible for a gelding to continue to have certain types of stallion characteristics even several years after castration, particularly if he was castrated late in life and if he was a very aggressive stallion prior to castration.

Another commonly asked question is, "When can my gelding be turned back out with a group of mares?" We would suggest that the breeder wait at least 30 days before turning the gelding out with a group of mares. A study was conducted at Colorado State University in which stallions were castrated and then continued to be collected with an artificial vagina for several weeks after castration. Within a week after castration, the ejaculates contained only fluid from the accessory sex glands which contained an extremely low number of spermatozoa, all of which were dead. It is unlikely that, even as early as a week after castration, the gelding would be able to impregnate a mare. However, it is probably safest to wait at least 30 days and, hopefully by that time, the sex drive of the gelding will decrease to the point that he will not be interested in mounting and mating with a mare.

FACILITIES FOR BREEDING

The type of facility used for breeding depends upon the type of breeding (natural mating or artificial insemination) and the number of mares to be bred. The use of a clean

A Central Kentucky breeding shed.

pasture with good footing might be adequate for hand mating of a stallion to a relatively small number of mares. However, in most cases, a breeding shed that is covered, well-lighted, and with good footing is desirable. A typical breeding area should be at least 400 square feet (20 x 20) and preferably as much as 40 x 40. The

A controlled breeding in which the stallion is presented to the mare,
then allowed to mount. Note the number of breeding shed
personnel and the twitch and protective covering on the mare.

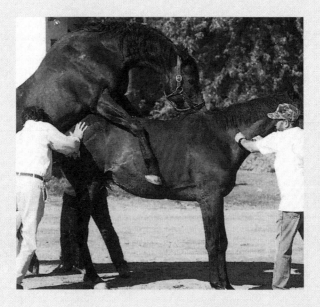

An outdoor breeding requiring fewer handlers (above); another kind of breeding (below), in which the stallion is presented to a tease mare...

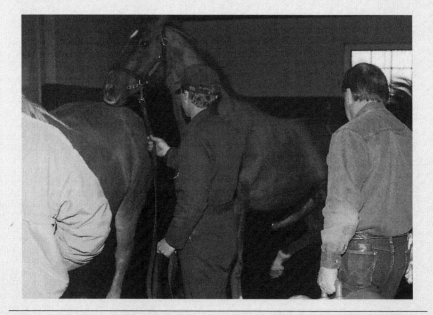

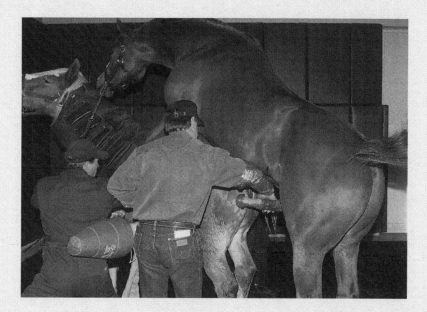

...allowed to mount (above), then diverted into an artificial vagina (below).

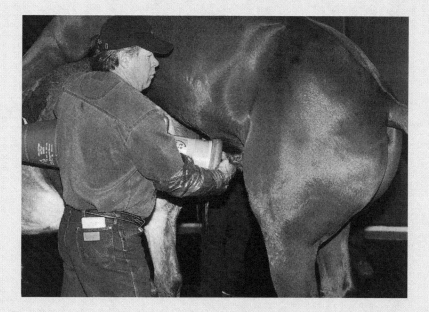

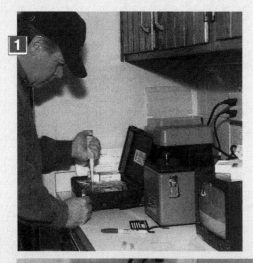

1) The author putting a semen specimen on a slide; 2) checking sperm motility and morphology on video microscope; 3) and putting specimen in the sperm counter.

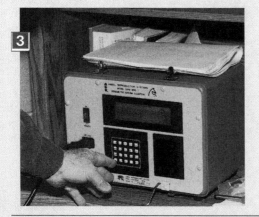

Some stallions have a tendency to bite (above); stallions should always be led with a shank that is at least 12 feet long and by someone who is not fearful.

Exercise is important for stallions, and farms can use various methods, including putting a horse on a mechanical walker. Note the use of bell boots and wraps (above) to protect the stallion's legs from injury.

A stallion enjoying a romp in his paddock (above); safety considerations for turn out include fencing with the posts on the outside (below).

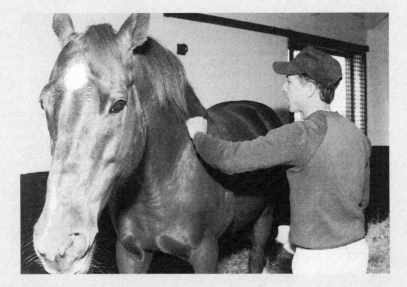

Grooming should be an
important part of a stallion's
daily routine.

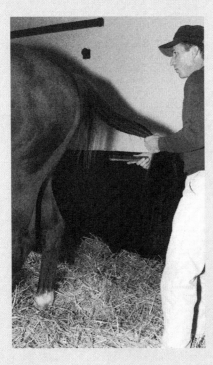

primary consideration should always be safety of the animal and personnel. The doors into the breeding shed should be at least 10 feet wide and 14 feet high, with a 14-foot ceiling. The flooring of the breeding shed is a matter of personal preference, but might include such elaborate material as rubber bricks or shredded rubber, tan bark, or Fibar. If one is to use inexpensive materials such as wood shavings, sawdust, pea gravel, or sand, then the area should be dampened so that the amount of dust is minimized. The breeding shed also should include a raised area so that animals of disproportionate size can be mated. Furthermore, the area of the breeding shed should include a padded tease rail for stimulation of the stallion, an area for washing the stallion's penis, and an area for breeding. One should consider a flow pattern which would minimize any injury to the personnel.

For artificial insemination, the breeding shed should include a phantom that is situated with the possibility of placing a mare parallel to the phantom. This is sometimes needed in order to encourage the stallion to mount the phantom. A head should be placed on the phantom for two reasons: 1) to prevent the stallion from going over the front of the phantom,

A breeding shed should be covered, well-lighted, and have good footing.

A mare in stocks.

and 2) as a possible stimulus to the stallion. If possible, a window from the breeding shed to the laboratory is desirable. This also can include a passageway in which the semen sample can be handed into the laboratory without tracking dirt into the laboratory. Some breeding sheds also include an area for observation for visitors.

Stallions slow to obtain an erection and mount a mare sometimes are stimulated by being housed in a small, safe enclosure within the breeding shed, so that they can observe other stallions breeding.

For artificial inseminations, mares should be placed in stocks and these stocks should be close to the laboratory. The most common mistake in constructing stocks is they are made too long or too wide. Breeding stocks are best made

A dedicated lab for semen evaluation.

out of pipe and should be six-feet long and approximately 30-inches wide. The flooring in the breeding shed should be a non-skid surface that can be disinfected. It is best to have a place beside or in front of the mares where the foals can be held while the mare is being inseminated.

The laboratory for semen evaluation should be a dedicated facility that is clean and dust free. Space should be available for storage of the artificial vaginas and liners and room for preparation of the artificial vagina. In addition, the lab should have enough counter space to hold a sperm counter, microscope, and possibly incubators. The equipment should be arranged in such a way that the artificial vagina would be brought into the laboratory, the collection bottle removed, and a clean specimen cup or graduate cylinder taken from the incubator for measurement of gel-free volume. The samples then should be evaluated for motility using a phase-contrast microscope and some form of counting device used to determine the number of sperm per milliliter. If possible, windows in the laboratory should face the palpation shed so that one can communicate with the staff. A slide-through window allows the semen sample to be passed from the laboratory into the insemination room.

CHAPTER 5

Sexual Behavior of the Stallion

NORMAL SEXUAL BEHAVIOR

Not until one has had the agony of handling a stallion with abnormal sexual behavior does that individual truly appreciate a stallion with normal sexual behavior. Breeders and veterinarians who have stood for hours waiting for a stallion to obtain an erection and ejaculate can certainly appreciate a stallion with good sexual behavior. Normal sexual behavior includes obtaining an erection within two to three minutes of being exposed to a mare in estrus. This stallion is then able to maintain that erection and, when present-

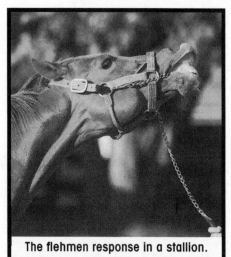

The flehmen response in a stallion.

ed to the mare, mount, and ejaculate after only one or two mounts. Stallions which have normal sexual behavior can be hand mated to one to three mares per day, or ejaculate into an artificial vagina every other day throughout the entire breeding season.

MASTURBATION

Many breeders are concerned when they see a stallion with an erection moving its penis up toward the body wall and down. This is commonly referred to as masturbation. The reason breeders become concerned with this behavior is that they think the stallion will become sexually satiated and therefore sex drive will decrease and/or a stallion will ejaculate and sperm numbers will be lower the next time the stallion is asked to breed or ejaculate into an artificial vagina. Sue McDonnell at the University of Pennsylvania has observed both domesticated and free-running stallions and noted that masturbation occurs with equal frequency in free-running and confined stallions at the rate of once every one to three hours in undisturbed animals. However, ejaculation is very seldom observed. The incidence of spontaneous erection or masturbation does not appear to be associated with confinement nor does it affect fertility.

AT A GLANCE

- A normal stallion will obtain an erection within two to three minutes of exposure to a mare in estrus.

- A normal stallion can be hand mated to one to three mares a day or ejaculate into an artificial vagina every other day throughout the breeding season.

- Masturbation is normal in domesticated and free-running stallions.

- Mismanagement is the most common cause of abnormal sexual behavior.

Many breeders and veterinarians become disturbed with this behavior and attempt to inhibit the behavior by putting a stallion ring on the penis of the stallion, which prevents erection, and/or strapping a brush on the belly of the stallion in order to discourage movement of the penis against the belly of the stallion.

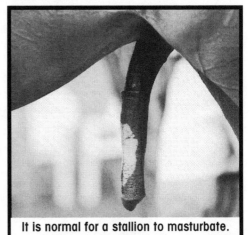

It is normal for a stallion to masturbate.

Both of these techniques are extremely detrimental to the stallion's well being. Many stallions have been rendered infertile through the use of a stallion ring and/or brush on the belly.

In most cases, there would appear to be no reason to become alarmed if the stallion exhibits this type of behavior. This should be considered normal behavior for a sexually mature stallion.

FREQUENCY OF BREEDING

One of the most commonly asked question is — How many mares can a stallion breed? If the stallion has normal testis size, the most important factor determining the number of mares a stallion can breed is his sexual behavior. Stallions in a pasture mating system have been known to mate several times a day. In a study by Bristol et al. (1982), researchers demonstrated that the criteria for a stallion breeding a mare

Frequency of breeding depends on the individual stallion.

in pasture is the mare's willingness to stand. In this study, a mare often was bred several days before ovulation. Thus, the misconception that a stallion is smart enough to breed a mare once only at the time of ovulation is not substantiated. The frequency at which stallions breed in a pasture setting is considerably higher than that of those which are hand-mated. The exact reason for this is unknown but could be due to a variety of mares in estrus at a given time and the lack of any man-made restraint. Apparently the restraint we impose when hand mating or artificially collecting semen alters sexual behavior. Because of the increased frequency of breeding during pasture mating, most pasture-breeding stallions are housed with no more than 50 mares.

The Thoroughbred breed is the largest horse breed that does not allow artificial insemination. All of the mares in this breed are hand mated by natural breeding. A stallion with normal-sized testicles and good sexual behavior can be used once or twice a day and, in many cases, three times a day during the peak of the breeding season. It is important to space the breedings throughout the day such that some mares are bred in the morning and some in the afternoon, and, if three matings are required per day, the last matings are done in the evening. The typical number of mares mated to a Thoroughbred stallion would be approximately 40 to 50, although some of the popular Thoroughbred stallions are breeding 80 to 100 mares in one breeding season and those stallions which service mares in both the Northern and Southern Hemispheres may breed as many as 200 mares each year by natural mating.

ARTIFICIAL INSEMINATION

The majority of breeds allow artificial insemination, which has many advantages for the stallion. With artificial insemination, a stallion can be collected once every other day and, on the average, 10 to 15 mares can be bred with each collection. The other important advantage of artificial insemination is that the stallion can be mounted on a phantom mare, thus preventing

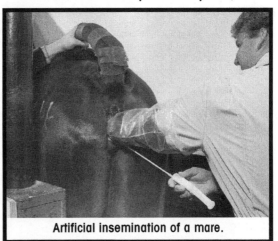
Artificial insemination of a mare.

any chance of the stallion being kicked during the mating process. Additionally, the semen can be added to an extender containing antibiotics and, thus, minimize any chance of the mare becoming infected from bacteria that might be contained in the semen. With artificial insemination, the number of mares which can be bred within a given year is increased, with a book of 100 to 200 mares in a breeding season being quite feasible.

COMMON BEHAVIORAL PROBLEMS

One of the most common causes of infertility in stallions is abnormal sexual behavior. The most common cause of abnormal sexual behavior is mismanagement. Therefore it is extremely important to train a stallion properly to ensure that he develops normal behavior. Ideally, stallions should not be used for breeding until at least three years of age. This has nothing to do with lack of testicular tissue or sperm numbers, but has much to do with development of good

Stallions should not be isolated.

sexual behavior. Those stallions used at two years of age are more likely to develop such bad habits as mounting without an erection, failure to obtain an erection, and excessive biting of the mare. Many breeders are anxious to obtain offspring from their young stallion, and thus attempt to breed a few mares when the stallion is two years old. If this is to occur, then the breeder should be very aware of any indications of abnormal behavior. Certainly a 2-year-old stallion should not be used for more than five or 10 mares, regardless of his apparent maturity and sexual behavior.

Other management practices that could lead to abnormal sexual behavior in older stallions include overuse, particularly in the fall and winter, unnecessary roughness, housing stallions in complete isolation, lack of exercise and, most importantly, being kicked during the breeding process. Stallions certainly should not be allowed to endanger any of the personnel, but excessive roughness during the breeding process can discourage the stallion and induce poor sexual behavior. Stallions should be housed where they can see other horses. Housing in complete isolation can result in poor libido of the stallion. Stallions which experience difficulty in obtaining an erection should be exposed to a variety of mares in estrus and given the opportunity to select the mare that is stimulatory. Furthermore, these stallions should have a blood sample taken and have a variety of hormones measured to determine if the lack of sex drive is due to a hormonal dysfunction. Stallions which experience difficulty in mounting and entering the mare might be suffering from physical pain in the hocks, stifle, or back area. These stallions should be examined by a veterinarian to determine if there is any abnormality resulting in this mounting difficulty. Another possible reason for a stallion failing to enter a mare is his fear of being kicked while in the mare. Generally, stallions which have been kicked are psychologically impotent. Retraining this type of stallion is difficult and generally requires mounting the stallion on a phantom and collecting semen or mounting the stallion on a mare in estrus that he has selected. This approach improves the stallion's confidence and, in most cases, will restore his ability to mount, enter, and ejaculate. One of the most common types of abnormal behavior is mounting, entering, and thrusting, but dismounting prior to ejaculation. Again, these stallions generally have been kicked during the breeding process and associate the act of ejaculation with being kicked. Once again, these stallions must be retrained to gain confidence before they will establish normal sexual behavior.

REFERENCES

Bristol et al., 1982

CHAPTER 6
What Affects Reproductive Performance?

SEASON

One major factor affecting reproductive performance of the stallion is season. Although the stallion does not show dramatic seasonal changes as the mare does, there are some very distinct hormonal, behavioral, and physiological changes that occur during the fall and winter. The stallion, like the mare, is considered a long-day breeder and peak sperm output occurs from April to June, corresponding with the mare's physiologic (natural) breeding season. The seasonal changes in the stallion are controlled by alterations in hormone levels. During the fall and winter when the day length is decreased, GnRH secretion from the hypothalamus and LH and FSH secretion from the pituitary are suppressed. This suppression of the hypothalamus and pituitary results in lowered levels of testosterone from the testes. The end result is lowered numbers of

Sperm production declines in the fall and winter.

spermatozoa being produced during the fall and winter.

The number of Sertoli cells in the testes is also influenced by season. Sertoli cell numbers in testes of adult stallion are greater during the breeding season than during the nonbreeding season. Approximately half the sperm numbers are obtained in an ejaculate collected during January as compared to an ejaculate collected during the peak of the breeding season (April to May). In addition, the volume of the ejaculate is reduced by approximately 50% in the fall and winter, but the quality of semen, based on progressive motility, does not change throughout the various months of the year. This maintenance of consistent semen quality throughout the year is contingent upon the stallion voiding the excess spermatozoa in the

AT A GLANCE

- Peak sperm output occurs from April to June; sperm production declines during the fall and winter.

- Stallions do not become sexually mature until age 5 or 6.

- It is not advisable to breed 2-year-old stallions.

- Sperm numbers in the ejaculate correlate directly to testicle size.

- Anabolic steroids can decrease testis size, sperm output, and semen quality.

urine. Those stallions which accumulate an excessive number of spermatozoa in the storage areas could have poor spermatozoal motility in the initial ejaculates after several days or weeks of sexual rest.

Season also has a dramatic effect on sexual behavior. The number of mounts required per ejaculation and the time required for a stallion to

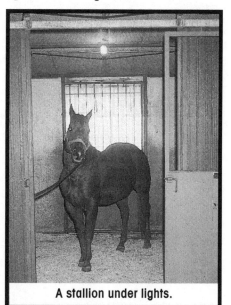

A stallion under lights.

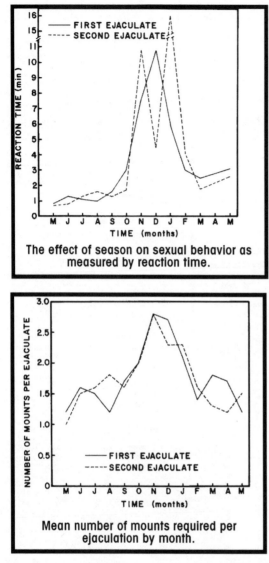

The effect of season on sexual behavior as measured by reaction time.

Mean number of mounts required per ejaculation by month.

obtain an erection, mount the mare, and ejaculate is more than doubled in the fall and winter compared to summer. Although stallions produce sperm throughout the year, attempts to continue to breed stallions year round might have adverse effects on sexual behavior.

Artificial photoperiod has been used to hasten the onset of peak sperm production. Stallions placed under 16 hours of light beginning December 1 will have maximum sperm production in February and March, as opposed to the usual peak production of sperm in May and June. This is only an advantage if one wants to breed most of the mares early in the year and shorten the breeding season, since sperm output of stallions exposed to artificial light declines earlier in the breeding season than it does for stallions under natural photoperiod.

Breeding of the same stallion in both the Northern and Southern Hemispheres has increased with some of the more popular Thoroughbred stallions. These stallions are asked to work year round and are exposed mostly to days of long photoperiod. Studies have shown that exposure of a stallion to 16 hours of light for an entire year still results in seasonal changes in sexual behavior and seminal characteristics.

AGE

The number of sperm the stallion is capable of producing is also influenced by the stallion's age. Too often a young horse is over-used and an older stallion is under-used. A stallion's age, because of its effect on testis development and function, is one of the most important factors affecting sperm production and

Effect of Age on Seminal Characteristics of Stallions			
	Age (yr)		
Characteristics[a]	**2 to 3 (7)[b]**	**4 to 6 (16)**	**9 to 16 (21)**
Seminal volume (ml)			
Gel	2.1	5.1	13.3
Gel-free	14.2	26.2	29.8
Total	16.2	31.4	43.2
Spermatozoa			
Conc (10⁶/ml)	120.4	160.9	161.3
Total (10⁹)	1.8	3.6	4.5
Motility (%)	55	63	60
pH	7.68	7.64	7.59

[a] Means of five successive ejaculates.
[b] Numbers in parentheses represent the number of stallions in each age group.

output and thus number of mares which can be bred. Number of sperm available for ejaculation depends upon sperm reserves in the tail of the epididymis, deferent ducts, and ampullae. Sperm reserves of sexually rested stallions increase with advancing age. Approximately twice the number of spermatozoa are present in the body of the epididymis from 10- to 16-year-old stallions than from 2- to 4-year-olds.

Seminal characteristics were compared among 2- to 3-, 4- to 6-, and 9- to 16-year-old stallions. Semen volume and sperm numbers were lower in ejaculates obtained from 2- to 3-year-old stallions than those from 4- to 6- and

Age influences sperm production.

9- to 16-year-olds. Most of the seminal characteristics were similar between stallions 4 to 6 and 9 to 16 years old. It would appear that the stallions does not become sexually mature until approximately five to six years of age. The number of sperm produced in a horse of any age is related to the size of the testicles. Testicular size in the stallion appears to increase steadily until the stallion is approximately 12 years of age. Although many 2-year-old stallions have sufficient sperm to breed several mares, we recommend that the stallion not be used as a 2-year-old, due to the possibility of acquiring abnormal sexual behavior. Even a 3-year-old stallion should have the number of mares it breeds monitored carefully. It is best to evaluate the breeding potential of the stallion each year prior to the breeding season in order to predict how many mares a stallion can handle successfully that breeding season. This is particularly true once stallions are 14 to 16 years of age.

TESTES SIZE AND CONSISTENCY

Sperm numbers in the ejaculate are directly correlated to the size of the stallion's testicles. Approximately 55% of the variation in sperm production can be accounted for by the size of the testicles. Stallion managers and veterinarians should measure the size of the stallion's testicles at least once a year, and preferably, once a month during the breeding season. There are two methods of measuring stallion testicles: a set of calipers (Animal Reproduction Systems, Chino, CA) or ultrasonographically measuring the stallion's testicles

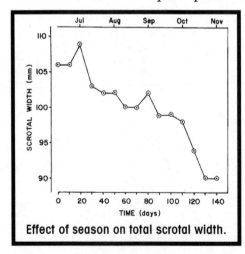

Effect of season on total scrotal width.

and using a formula published by Love et al. (1991) that calculates the volume of testicular tissue. This equation can be used to predict the number of spermatozoa that the stallion is capable of producing. A stallion's testicular size does not change due to ejaculation frequency, but does change due to season. Mean scrotal width decreases from 109 mm in July to 90 mm in November.

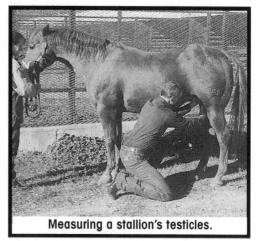
Measuring a stallion's testicles.

Not only should the testicles be measured, but their consistency or tone assessed. Both testicles should be positioned in the scrotum in a horizontal position. Each testicle should be positioned between the thumb and fingers by pushing the opposite testicle upward. Evidence of abnormal conditions should be detected, such as soft, mushy testes; excessively hard testes; ventral ribbing; rotation of testes in the scrotum; lobulation and constriction bands. Testicular abnormalities that are of concern can include a soft, mushy-feeling testicle. This could possibly indicate testicular degeneration or could indicate that the stallion received drugs such as anabolic steroids or testosterone. In contrast, very firm, rough-feeling testicles also are undesirable. These characteristics also could indicate testicular degeneration.

Top sire A.P. Indy was born a cryptorchid.

Stallions which have only one testicle descended in the scrotum are called cryptorchid stallions and the number of sperm they can produce is reduced. Although the remaining testicle can compensate by growing, the one testicle will never increase to a size that approximates a normal stallion with two testicles. In addition, stallions with only one testicle descended are more likely to develop aggressiveness and other forms of abnormal sexual behavior. If the testis and epididymis are both within the abdomen, the horse is termed a complete abdominal cryptorchid. Retained testes do not produce spermatozoa because of the elevated temperature within the body cavity.

Testicular descent into the scrotum is a very complex process. Therefore, causes of abnormal descent can be varied and difficult to document. Mechanical causes for abnormal testicular descent in stallions include over stretching of the gubernaculum cord, insufficient abdominal pressure, inadequate growth of the gubernaculum and related structures, inadequate dilation of the vaginal ring and inguinal canal for passage of the testis, and displacement of the testis into the pelvic cavity. Several studies have suggested a genetic basis for cryptorchidism in the horse. However definitive studies to determine the genetic basis for cryptorchidism in the stallion have not been conducted. Many breeds discourage the use of a cryptorchid stallion because of the possible inheritance of this developmental problem. For horses with one retained testis and one scrotal testis, a search for and removal of the retained testis should proceed castration of the descended testis.

FREQUENCY OF EJACULATION

Frequency of ejaculation is one of the most important factors affecting sperm output. As the frequency of ejaculation for artificial insemination or natural service increases, the number of spermatozoa per ejaculate decreases, providing frequency equals or exceeds one ejaculate every other day. If the stallion has an extremely high sex drive and can ejaculate several times per day, fertility could decline because he ejaculates insufficient numbers of sperm, particularly if used early in the breeding season.

A series of studies were conducted to determine how often stallions could be used in a natural service program and an artificial insemination program. The results of these studies demonstrated that the total number of sperm per ejaculate was the same whether stallions were collected six times per week or three times per week. In addition, the total sperm collected on a weekly basis was the same for stallions collected three versus six times per week. Based on these data, it was determined that collection frequency above every other day will not result in more sperm per week. Thus, the most efficient collection schedule for a stallion in an artificial insemination program is once every other day (Pickett et al. 1989).

For a natural mating program, the number of mares which can be bred in a given day depends on the stallion's sexual behavior and testis size. Assuming the stallion has been bred at least once a day for 10 days, the number of spermatozoa in the ejaculate after this 10-day period is essentially what the stallion is capable of producing (daily sperm production). We know that approximately 100 to 500 million progressively motile spermatozoa are needed for maximum reproductive efficiency. Therefore, if the number of sperm in the stallion's ejaculate is several billion, then more than likely, the limiting factor as to the number of mares the stallion can breed is based on his willingness to breed. Generally, stallions can be used once or twice a day in a natural breeding program, and possibly three times per day for a limited period of time. Any time the stallion is given one or two days of sexual rest, then sperm numbers will accumulate in his sperm reserve.

HORMONE INJECTIONS

Anabolic steroids are testosterone-like hormones often given to young stallions in an attempt to increase muscle mass and size. Because all anabolic steroids have some testosterone-like properties, they have the ability to decrease LH secretion from the pituitary. This ultimately results in decreased stimulation of the testis by LH and a decrease in testosterone. Continued treatment of a stallion with anabolic steroids results in a decrease in testis size, sperm output, and semen quality. Anabolic steroid administration is particularly detrimental when given to young males prior to the time of puberty (weanlings and yearlings). It is likely that, if sufficient anabolic steroids are given to young horses prior to the

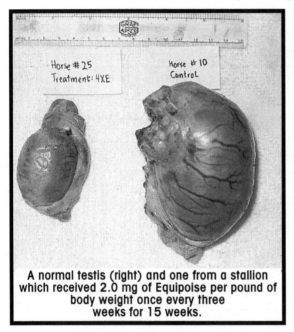

time of puberty, development of the testis will be impaired for life. In contrast, administration of anabolic steroids to older stallions will cause temporary changes in testis size, sperm output, and semen quality, but after cessation of treatment, testicular size, sperm output, and semen quality will improve in three to five months after the end of treatment. Many times,

A normal testis (right) and one from a stallion which received 2.0 mg of Equipoise per pound of body weight once every three weeks for 15 weeks.

stallions which have been shown or raced heavily have very poor testicular consistency and semen quality during their first breeding season but eventually might improve in subsequent years. Needless to say, administration of anabolic steroids is not recommended at any age.

Testosterone injections have been advocated for stallions with low sex drive. However, studies have demonstrated that injection of testosterone into stallions also can be detrimental due to the negative effect on LH secretion. Once LH levels fall, testosterone produced by the testicles also is decreased.

This, again, results in low levels of testosterone at the level of the testicle and decreased sperm production and semen quality. Furthermore, there is no strong evidence that injecting testosterone into a stallion will improve his sexual behavior. More appropriately, a stallion with poor sexual behavior should have blood drawn and hormonal levels measured. If, in fact, testosterone is lower than normal, then the hormone gonadotropin-releasing hormone (GnRH) should be given. This hormone is more appropriate since it simulates normal hormonal events in a stallion. Upon injecting GnRH, the pituitary is stimulated to produce LH which subsequently stimulates the testes to produce testosterone. A veterinarian should be consulted in determining the regimen for treating a stallion with GnRH. Typically, several pulses of GnRH are released in the stallion, under natural conditions, each day. Therefore, in order to simulate the natural secretion of GnRH, this hormone should be given several times per day.

Stallions used for racing or showing are often very aggressive and difficult to manage when around other stallions or mares. Thus, vet-

A stallion outfitted with a GnRH pump.

erinarians are often asked — How can one suppress sexual behavior in the stallion temporarily during the training, racing, or showing events? ReguMate® is an orally active synthetic progesterone compound used to suppress estrous behavior in the mare. The mechanism in the mare is through suppression of LH levels. ReguMate® has been shown to suppress sexual behavior in the stallion. Administration of ReguMate® at twice the recommended dose for mares (approximately 20 ml/day) resulted in decreased sperm output, semen quality, and testis size after approximately 45 days of continued administration. Decreased LH secretion, however, was detected within a few days after the initiation of ReguMate® treatment. Other studies also have demonstrated an effect of ReguMate® on seminal characteristics. Breeders have stated that ReguMate® takes "the edge off the stallion," allowing stallions to be more manageable during training, racing, or showing.

The mechanism for decreased testis size, sperm output, and semen quality in stallions receiving ReguMate® appears to be the same as that of anabolic steroids and testosterone, i.e., the suppression in LH secretion. Breeders should be concerned with using ReguMate® on extremely young, prepubertal stallions, since there is a possibility of suppressing development of the reproductive system. Treatment of older stallions appears to have only a temporary effect on these testicular and seminal characteristics and several months after cessation of treatment, these characteristics improve. Certainly, one should not attempt to administer ReguMate® and use the stallion as a breeding stallion at the same time.

REFERENCES

Pickett, BW, Squires, EL, and McKinnon, AO. Procedures for collection, evaluation, and utilization of stallion semen for artificial insemination. Colorado State Univ. Animal Reprod. Lab Bull. No. 03 (1987).

Pickett, BW, Amann, RP, McKinnon, AO, Squires, EL, and Voss, JL. Management of the stallion for maximum reproductive efficiency, II. Colorado State Univ. Animal Reprod. Lab Bull. No. 05 (1989).

Love, CC, Garcia, MC, Riera, FR, and Kenney, RM. 1991. Evaluation of measures taken by ultrasonography and calipers to estimate testicular volume and predict daily sperm output in the stallion. *J. Reprod. Fertility.* 44: 99.

Squires, EL, Badzinski, SL, Amann, RP, McCue, PM, and Nett, TM. 1997. Effects of altrenogest on total scrotal width, seminal characteristics, concentrations of LH and testosterone, and sexual behavior of stallions. *Theriogenology.* 48: 313-328.

CHAPTER 7

Cooled and Frozen Semen

The acceptance of artificial insemination (AI) by the majority of breed registries has had dramatic effects on the horse industry. However, the recent acceptance of cooled, transported semen by most breeds and the acceptance of frozen-thawed semen by some breeds will have even more influence on horse breeding over the next decade. The ability to preserve semen in a cooled or frozen state provides more opportunity and flexibility for horse breeding.

The major advantage of cooled semen is the elimination of the cost and stress of shipping a mare and/or foal to a breeding farm and a reduction in cash outlay for mare care. Leaving the mare at home also reduces the possibility of disease transmission through exposure of the mare or foal to a new environment.

The disadvantages of cooled semen are the costs involved in collecting, packaging, and shipping the semen container to the mare owner and the increased veterinary costs for mare examination and hormonal control of the mare's cycle. Also, semen from all stallions does not survive cooling and shipping.

HANDLING COOLED SEMEN

For proper handling of cooled semen, a laboratory

equipped with clean equipment and supplies should be available. Initial handling and evaluation of stallion semen is the same, whether the semen will be used immediately or whether it will be cooled. It is essential that the number of spermatozoa per milliliter be determined, as well as the percentage of spermatozoa that are progressively motile. Ideally, each shipment will contain 1 billion progressively motile spermatozoa. There are several factors to consider when pack-

AT A GLANCE

- Cooled and frozen semen provide more opportunity and flexibility for horse breeding.

- Advantages include elimination of shipping costs for the mare and reduced exposure to disease.

- Disadvantages include the cost of collecting and shipping semen and lower conception rates when using frozen semen.

aging a dose of semen for shipment. The two most important factors are concentration of the spermatozoa per milliliter and the dilution of extender with semen. Samples that are too concentrated or too diluted result in poor viability and reduced fertility. A rule of thumb is to estimate the motility of the sample and determine the volume of semen needed to provide 1 billion progressively motile spermatozoa. Add this volume of raw semen to enough extender to provide at least a 3:1 dilution (3 parts extender to 1 part semen) and/or dilute to a concentration of approximately 25 million motile spermatozoa per milliliter. If one takes a volume of raw semen containing 1 billion motile spermatozoa and adds enough extender to provide a final volume of 40 ml, then a concentration of 25 million motile spermatozoa/ml would always be obtained. However, if a dilution of 3:1 is not obtained, then more extender will have to be added.

The semen packaging system that has been tested most extensively and one that is highly recommended is the Equitainer manufactured by Hamilton Thorne. This is a passive cooling unit that allows semen to be cooled at a slow rate from 37°C to 5°C. For shipment of semen, an extender composed of nonfat dried milk solids, glucose, and antibiotics should be used. The extender, E-Z Mixin CST (Animal Reproduction Laboratories, Chino, CA), containing the antibiotic amikacin, is designed specifically for shipping equine semen. The E-Z Mixin CST should be added to the semen and the extended semen poured into a baby bottle liner or a whirlpack bag. The excess air should be expressed out of the baby bottle liner by twisting the top. The sealed bag of extended semen containing 1 billion progressively motile sper-

The Equitainer, used to transport cooled semen.

matozoa then is placed into the specimen cup. The extended semen should be wrapped in one or two ballast bags to provide the appropriate total liquid volume of 120 to 170 milliliters. The specimen cup containing semen and ballast bags then is placed inside the isothermalizer, which is placed inside the Equitainer on top of the coolant cans. The coolant cans have been in a deep freeze for at least 24 hours prior to being placed in the Equitainer. The extended semen in the Equitainer will be cooled to 5°C during transit. An information sheet should be placed on top of the semen, which contains the stallion's name, date, time of seminal collection, date of seminal collection, volume of raw semen, volume of extender, type of extender used, and number of spermatozoa shipped per dose. The Equitainer is then shipped by commercial airlines or courier service.

Factors that affect the fertility of cooled semen include storage time, cooling rates, storage temperature, dilution, antibiotics, and timing of insemination. If properly diluted, semen from most stallions can be stored for 24 hours and for some stallions, 48 hours. Semen that is cooled too rapidly from 37°C to 5°C results in cold shock. Semen must be cooled very slowly (less than or equal to 3° per minute) between the temperatures of 20°C and about 8°C. This is the temperature range of sperm's susceptibility to cold shock. Studies have shown that storage of semen is better at 5°C than 0°C. Based on numerous studies, if semen is to be used within 12 hours of collection, it can be stored at either 20°C or 5°C. However, for storage longer than 12 hours, semen must be cooled slowly to 5°C. Storage at 4°C to 5°C is better for maintenance of equine spermatozoa than 0°C or 2°C.

Little information is available on the proper timing of insemination of cooled semen to maximize fertility. However, it is quite likely that timing of insemination of cooled semen is more critical than that of fresh semen. It is recommended that mares be inseminated with cooled semen within 24 hours prior to ovulation or within six hours after ovulation.

FROZEN SEMEN

There are several advantages to the use of frozen semen over that of fresh or cooled semen:

1) Semen can be stored indefinitely in a liquid nitrogen container.

2) The breeding season can continue, even when the stallion is at a performance event, ill, or recovering from an injury.

3) Differences in the breeding season between Northern and Southern hemispheres would no longer pose a problem.

4) The semen would only have to be shipped once to the breeding farm and would be available throughout the breeding season.

The major disadvantage with the use of frozen semen is the considerable technology and skill required for processing, packaging, freezing, and inseminating. The most serious disadvantage of frozen semen is the reduced pregnancy rates obtained with semen from most stallions. It is likely that, as the technology improves, the use of frozen semen will increase and that of cooled semen will decrease. However, new and improved techniques are needed for minimizing the damage to semen during the freezing and thawing processes.

The major steps in freezing stallion spermatozoa include dilution, centrifugation to remove seminal plasma and concentration of the spermatozoa, resuspension in a freezing extender containing a cryoprotectant, cooling to -120°C and storage in liquid nitrogen at -196°C. Success in cryopreservation of stallion spermatozoa depends on a complex series of interactions among extenders, cryoprotectants, and cooling and warming rates.

The major components that damage spermatozoa during the freezing and thawing process include ice crystal formation and the toxic effects of the extender components. The goal is to dehydrate the spermatozoa successfully during the cooling process using salts, sugars, and cryoprotectants such

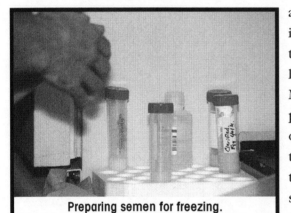

Preparing semen for freezing.

as glycerol without exposing the spermatozoa to these components for too long of a period of time. Most equine semen is packaged in 0.5 ml straws or 4 or 5 ml straws prior to cooling over liquid nitrogen vapor. Once the semen is frozen, it is maintained in liquid nitrogen at a temperature of -196°C. At this temperature, the semen can be maintained in a viable state indefinitely.

The major factor affecting the fertility of frozen-thawed equine spermatozoa appears to be the individual stallion. For unknown reasons, some stallions have spermatozoa that withstand the freezing and thawing process better than others. In general, if one froze semen from 100 different stallions, 25 would have frozen-thawed semen that provides a pregnancy rate of approximately 40-60% per cycle, 50 would have frozen-thawed spermatozoa that provide a pregnancy rate of 25-40% per cycle, and 25 of the stallions would have extremely low fertility with frozen-thawed spermatozoa (less than 25% per cycle).

Tremendous effort is going into developing techniques for freezing and thawing equine spermatozoa. It is likely that tremendous progress will be made in the next decade in developing these technologies. Development of procedures for assessing damage to the spermatozoon after freezing and thawing is an important prerequisite to the development of techniques for freezing equine spermatozoa. Unfortunately, spermatozoal motility of frozen-thawed equine spermatozoa is not a good indicator of fertility. Therefore, other laboratory tests are needed to assess the viability of frozen-thawed equine spermatozoa. These tests could be used to identify spermatozoa that have been severely damaged during the freezing and thawing proccss, thus preventing the breeder from using damaged spermatozoa. It is likely that numerous laboratory tests will be developed in the next several years that can be used to evaluate the various techniques for freezing and thawing equine spermatozoa.

FREQUENTLY ASKED QUESTIONS

1) *Should my breeding stallion be used as a teaser stallion?*

On many small farms, it is uneconomical to maintain an additional stallion just to be used as a teaser. Thus, if a breeding stallion enjoys teasing mares, i.e., attains an erection and maintains the erection during the teasing process, then there is nothing wrong with using a breeding stallion as a teaser.

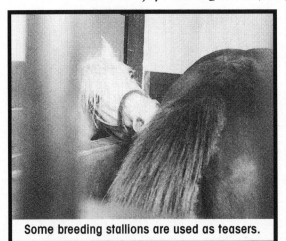
Some breeding stallions are used as teasers.

However, if semen is to be shipped, then teasing will increase the volume of the ejaculate and decrease the concentration, which is not good for shipping semen. Ideally, if a large number of mares is to be teased, it would be advantageous to purchase a tease horse that is aggressive and enjoys teasing.

2) *How many mares can my stallion breed?*
This would depend on whether one was going to breed a

stallion naturally or by artificial insemination. Generally, the single most important limiting factor as to how many mares a stallion can breed is his sex drive. If the stallion has normal testicles and good sex drive, he probably can handle being bred naturally once or twice, or possibly even three times per day on occasion.

With artificial insemination, the stallion should be collected only every other day and under these conditions it would not be difficult to breed a stallion to more than 100 mares.

3) What can I give my "slow working" stallion to increase his sex drive?

First, I would draw blood from the stallion to determine if the cause of his low sex drive is due to hormonal levels. If testosterone is low, then the safest therapy would be to administer gonadotropin-releasing hormone (GnRH). There might be other management changes that can be used to increase the stallion's sexual behavior, such as housing the stallion where

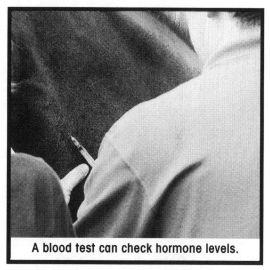

A blood test can check hormone levels.

he can see other stallions and mares and/or forced exercise.

4) What effect does artificial light have on the stallion?

Artificial light can be initiated in December and used to induce increased testicular size, sperm output, and enhanced sexual behavior in the months of February and March. However, unlike the mare, these same parameters begin to decrease by May, June, or July. Thus, light can be used to induce increased sperm numbers, but this is only an advantage if a large number of mares are going to be bred very early in the breeding season.

5) My stallion typically has extremely good quality semen, but on today's collection all the sperm were dead. What went wrong?

More than likely there was a mistake made in the collection process. This could have resulted from too warm of an artificial vagina, failing to lower the artificial vagina during the ejaculation process, or not emptying the water out of the artificial vagina quickly enough after ejaculation. It might also be a result of improper handling of the collection equipment. Alternatively, the poor quality semen might be the beginning of a series of poor quality ejaculates due to an insult to the testis and/or the stallion having a high fever in the last several weeks or months.

There are disadvantages to competing breeding stallions.

6) Can I use my stallion as a breeding stallion and still continue to compete with the stallion?

Generally it would be best to make a decision to use the stallion as either a breeding stallion or a show horse. There are several disadvantages in trying to use the stallion as both a show and breeding horse. Obviously if the horse is being shown or competing in events, it is extremely undesirable for the horse to obtain an erection and show interest in mares. The techniques used to inhibit sexual behavior during competition are sometimes adverse to the stallion's breeding performance. These might include such harsh treatments as slapping the stallion on the penis to make the stallion withdraw the penis into the sheath. Other types of treatments might include administering ReguMate® to the stallion to suppress sexual behavior. Both of these types of treatments certainly would adversely affect the stallion's re-productive perform-ance. The other disadvantage is that the stallion is away from the breeding farm at critical times. This results in several mares not being bred at the appropriate time and could, in fact, extend the breeding season.

Ideally, one would compete with the stallion until his show career is finished, then retire the stallion to a breeding farm setting. Another alternative would be to freeze significant quantities of semen from the stallion, castrate the stallion, and show the stallion as a gelding.

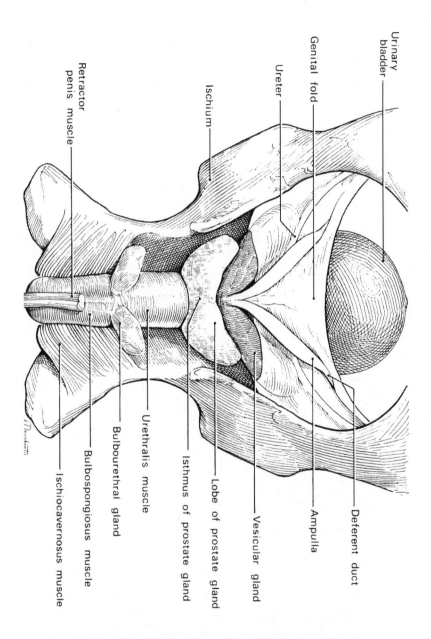

Dorsal view of the pelvic portion of the reproductive tract.

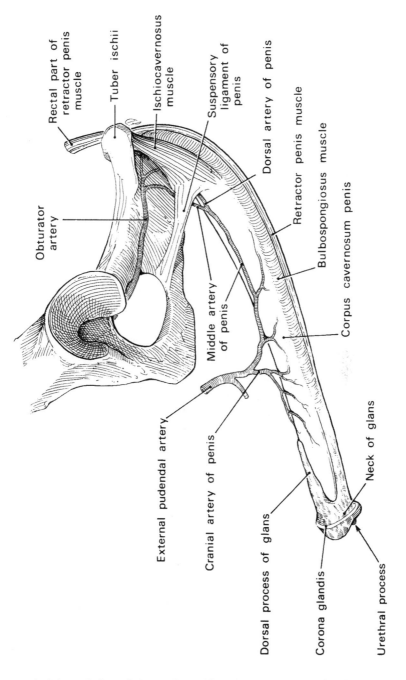

Left lateral view of the penis and its attachment to the ischium.

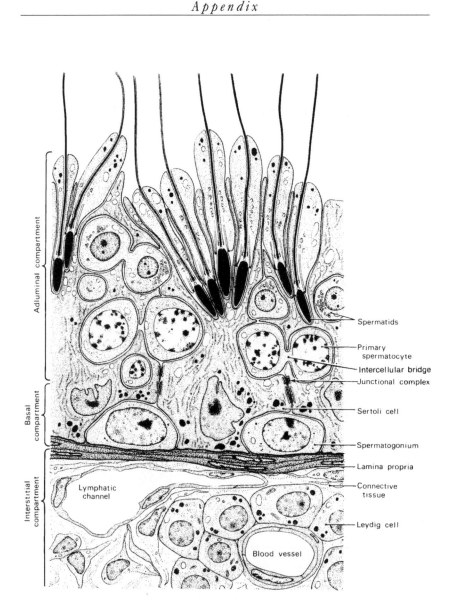

A section of the stallion seminiferous tubule showing the relationship of germ cells and adjacent Sertoli cells in the seminiferous epithelium. Formation of a spermatozoon starts near the basement membrane, where a spermatogonium divides to form other spermatogonia and ultimately primary spermatocytes that are moved to a position away from the basement membrane but below the junctional complex between adjacent Sertoli cells.

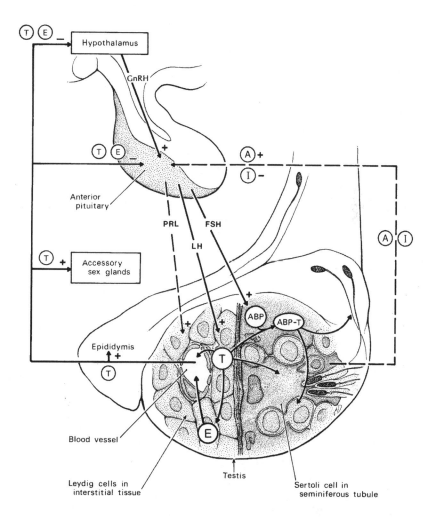

The interrelationship of pituitary hormones acting on Leydig and Sertoli cells of the seminiferous tubules, and feedback control of gonadal hormones of the hypothalamus and anterior lobe of the pituitary gland. Adequate concentrations of testosterone and FSH must be present to stimulate Sertoli cells to produce an environment appropriate for normal spermatogenesis.

A = activin, ABP = androgen binding proteins, E = estradiol or other estrogens, GnRH = gonadotropin releasing hormone, I = inhibin, LH = luteinizing hormone, FSH = follicle stimulating hormone, PRL = prolactin, and T= testosterone.

Cryptorchid — A stallion with a testis that has not descended into the scrotum.

Epididymis — An oblong organ attached to each testis. Its function is to aid in maturation and storage of spermatozoa.

Germ cell — An egg or spermatozoa or one of their precursors.

Hypothalamus — That portion of the brain involved in secreting Gonadotropin-releasing hormone (GnRH).

Inguinal canal — The passage between the abdomen and the vaginal cavity that surrounds the spermatic cord in the adult male.

Leydig cells — The interstitial cells of the seminiferous tubules.

Libido — Sexual desire.

Masturbation — Self manipulation of the penis with or without the occurrence of ejaculation.

Morphology — The form or structure of organisms or part of organisms.

Pathogenic bacteria — Bacteria that are capable of causing uterine infection in mares.

Photoperiod — The period of time each day that an animal is exposed to either natural or artificial light.

Progressive motility — The percentage of spermatozoa that are traveling in a straight line.

Puberty — The period in which the stallion first becomes capable of sexual reproduction.

ReguMate® — An orally active progesterone-like compound

used to control estrus in mares.

Seminal — Pertaining to, containing, or consisting of semen.

Sertoli cells — The somatic cells within the seminiferous tubules that provide the appropriate environment for development and differentiation of germ cells.

Sperm reserves — The reservoir of sperm that are stored in the tail of the epidymis, ductus deferens, and ampullae.

Spermatogenesis — The process of formation of spermatozoa.

Spermatogonia — Undifferentiated male germ cells.

Spermatozoal concentration — Number of spermatozoa per milliliter of semen.

Tunica albugiea — A dense, white connective tissue that covers and contains the testis.

INDEX

RECOMMENDED READINGS

Pickett, BW, Amann, RP, McKinnon, AO, Squires, EL, and Voss, JL. Management of the Stallion for Maximum Reproductive Efficiency, II. Colorado State University Animal Reproduction Laboratory Bulletin No. 05. 1989.

Pickett, BW, Squires, EL, and McKinnon, AO. Procedures for Collection, Evaluation, and Utilization of Stallion Semen for Artificial Insemination. Colorado State University Animal Reproduction Laboratory Bulletin No. 03. 1987.

Squires, EL, Pickett, BW, Vanderwall, DK, McCue, PM, and Bruemmer, JE. Cooled and Frozen Stallion Semen. Colorado State University Animal Reproduction Laboratory Bulletin No. 09. 1999.

McKinnon, AO, and Voss, JL. *Equine Reproduction*. Philadelphia: Lea & Febiger, 1993.

McDonnell, S. *Understanding Horse Behavior*. Lexington, Ky: The Blood-Horse Publications, Inc. 1999.

Schweizer, CM. *Understanding the Broodmare*. Lexington, Ky: The Blood-Horse Publications, Inc. 1998.

Stallion sites on the Internet

The Horse: Your Online Guide To Equine Health Care:
http://www.thehorse.com

The American Association of Equine Practitioner's archived list
of horse articles:
http://www.aaep.org/client.htm

Colorado State University's equine reproduction services page:
http://www.cvmbs.colostate.edu/cvmbs/rcsu.html

The Equine Research Centre, Guelph, Ontario, Canada:
http://www.erc.on.ca

Cornell University's Equine Research Park that focuses on the
breeding and reproduction of horses:
http://web.vet.cornell.edu/public/cuerp/index.htm

Compendium of horse care and veterinary resources:
http://www.avma.org/netvet/horses.htm

Kentucky Equine Research. Once you log on to this address,
type in the key word "stallion" to pull up pertinent articles:
http://www.ker.com/library/index.html

Rural Industries Research and Development of Australia. Once
you access this address, type in the key word "stallion" for
pertinent articles:
http://www.usyd.edu.au/su/rirdc/search_engine.cgi

Picture Credits

CHAPTER 1
Suzanne Depp, 18; Anne M. Eberhardt, 19; Barbara D. Livington, 20;
Charlene Strickland, 20.

CHAPTER 2
Judy L. Marchman, 23; E.L. Squires, 24, 27, 29; Anne M. Eberhardt, 25; 26, 31;
Barbara D. Livingston, 30.

CHAPTER 3
Barbara D. Livingston, 32; Anne M. Eberhardt, 33-36, 40, 41;
E.L. Squires, 35, 38, 39.

CHAPTER 4
Barbara D. Livingston, 42, 45, 50; Anne M. Eberhardt, 43, 44, 49-56, 58;
Kendra Bond, 46; Suzie Picou-Oldham, 48; The Blood-Horse, 53, 57;
E. L. Squires, 58.

CHAPTER 5
Barbara D. Livingston, 60, 64; Anne M. Eberhardt, 61, 62;
U.S. Trotting Association, 63.

CHAPTER 6
Barbara D. Livingston, 66, 69; E. L. Squires, 67, 73.

CHAPTER 7
Jonathon F. Pycock, 80; Anne M. Eberhardt, 82.

FREQUENTLY ASKED QUESTIONS
Anne M. Eberhardt, 84, 85; Nanette T. Rawlins, 86.

EDITOR — JACQUELINE DUKE
COVER/BOOK DESIGN — SUZANNE C. DEPP
ILLUSTRATIONS — COLORADO STATE UNIVERSITY
COVER PHOTO — BARBARA D. LIVINGSTON

About the Author

E. L. Squires is a Professor in the Department of Physiology at Colorado State University. He received his Master's Degree in Reproductive Physiology from West Virginia University in 1971, and his Ph.D. in Endocrinology/Reproductive Physiology at the University of Wisconsin in 1974 under the direction of Dr. O. J. Ginther.

E. L. Squires, PhD

In 1984, Dr. Squires was awarded the Young Scientist Award from the American Society of Animal Science, and he was the recipient of the Colorado State University Faculty Alumni Award in 1985. He served as President of the Equine Nutrition and Physiology Society (ENPS) from 1985 to 1987. In 1989, he received the Distinguished Service in Equine Science Award from ENPS. He recently received the Fellows Award from ENPS.

Dr. Squires is supervisor of the Equine Reproduction Laboratory. His involvement includes teaching undergraduates, graduates, and veterinary students. Clinical duties include reproductive evaluation of mares and stallions, commercial embryo transfer, and freezing stallion semen. Dr. Squires was a pioneer in developing the techniques of embryo transfer. His most recent research has centered on development of assisted reproductive techniques such as oocyte maturation, *in vitro* fertilization, embryo freezing, and fertility of cooled and frozen semen. He currently is program director for the Preservation of Equine Genetics (PEG) program. This program, funded by private benefactors, includes numerous graduate students, post-doctoral students and visiting scientists, all working on developing assisted reproductive techniques for old mares and stallions.